WHO'S AFRAID
OF THE
DARK?

Best   Wishes

DEDICATION

*The author dedicates "Who's Afraid of the Dark" to the memory
of his younger brother, Kevin, who died in a tragic drowning
accident when aged 23. Kevin was not only a close friend but
also an inspiration because of his great sense of humour which
helped to lighten the darker days of the author's youth.
The book is also a tribute to the support of the author's father,
Dennis, his mother, Nellie, and his brothers, Leonard and Sean.*

The author wishes to acknowledge his indebtedness
to his wife Barbara for her tireless work in assisting with
the recording of his story by word processor and use of
computers; to his good friend Dr Barbara Watterson for
painstakingly reading the initial text; to Wendy Randall for
her encouragement and keeping him to a weekly schedule
of writing, and to Capt Andrew Douglas for his help in
supplying information and illustrations. Finally, The Royal
Bank of Scotland International who, in conjunction with
The Manx Experience have made this publication possible.

WHO'S AFRAID OF THE DARK?

Tom Glassey

THE ROYAL BANK OF SCOTLAND
——— INTERNATIONAL ———

The Manx Experience

The Manx Experience
45 Slieau Dhoo - Tromode Park - Douglas - Isle of Man - IM2 5LG

Published 2001 by The Manx Experience

Copyright © Tom Glassey 2001

ISBN 1 873120 55 9

**The author will make a donation
to St Vincent's School for the Blind, Liverpool from
royalties received from this publication.**

Printed in the Isle of Man by
Mannin Printing
(part of the Mannin Media Group Limited)
Spring Valley Industrial Estate - Braddan - Isle of Man - British Isles

Chapter One

I have no memory of ever being able to see. In 1955, at the age of two, I was diagnosed as having cancer of the retina *(Retinablastoma)* and I had both eyes removed. I never remember feeling hard done to as a child, it always seemed a perfectly natural state. The fact that I was a blind child didn't seem to make any difference to the kids in my neighbourhood, although I am sure that it did to the adults. From my earliest memories, the kids around me treated me as one of them. I don't know why, but I hardly remember bumping into anything as a child; indeed, I have many more scrapes now than I ever had then. I suppose being a blind child in Castletown, and the only blind child throughout the whole of the Isle of Man, made me a bit of a celebrity. Like me, my young playmates were totally unaware of the events that led up to my cancer. To their mums and dads, I was a story still unfolding.

In early September 1953, my dad stood waiting for the southbound bus from Douglas that was bringing my grandmother and aunt. They had travelled over from Ireland on the Isle of Man Steam Packet ferry from Dublin to Douglas, the Isle of Man's capital city, and were on the last seven miles of their journey to Ballasalla. My mother had come to the Island in 1950 from County Tipperary, to find work. By this time, she had not only found work but had also married my father and was now about to have her second son, yours truly. My older brother, Leonard, had been born the previous year, 1952. The bus stop was very near to our house and my dad waited on the opposite side of the road from it. Granny and Aunt Mary stepped down from the

From the family album . . .

Above: the author, aged two, is on the left, with his mother Nel holding baby brother Kevin. On the right is older brother Lennie, aged four.

Below: on the right is the author, now aged four, with his brother Lennie.

bus, then walked behind it and failed to spot the on-coming car. Auntie Mary was killed outright, and although Granny battled on for a short while, she died just a few weeks later. I was born a couple of days after this tragic event and whether it played any part in instigating the cancer I was about to endure, I have no way of knowing. I can only try to imagine how horrific these events must have been for my parents. People do find strength from the depths of despair; my parents certainly did, and they were going to have to find a lot more of it in the coming years.

I think I first started to hear the word school mentioned from about the age of four. I was sure it was only something that happened to other kids. I guess those around me had generally assumed that I would not be able to go to school and so maybe I was not conditioned for the almighty shock that was in store for me. My mother had already taken advice from the education authorities and they had suggested a special school for the blind in Liverpool. I was starting to hear the word Liverpool and school frequently, though I did not know at this stage where Liverpool was. I assumed it was just another place on the Island that I hadn't yet been to. It certainly did not occur to me that I would have to cross the sea and spend many months at a time away from home. I had thought I would go to school just like my brother Lenny; it would simply be a special school in a different place. I remember little of the build-up to my first trip to school; however, I remember vividly my first day there.

I was to travel to school on my first day with my mother and a wonderful family friend and neighbour, otherwise known as Auntie Dot. As a child I loved travelling on the bus, and often would accompany my mother to Douglas on a Saturday to do the family shopping. On the day I was to start school I remember nothing of the bus trip to Douglas. My first memories of that day are of walking along the pier of Douglas harbour holding my mother's hand and trailing the other hand along the harbour chains. I can recall hearing the swish of the small waves washing against the pier and dreading having to paddle out to the boat; but I comforted myself with the thought that I could not see my mother and Auntie Dot paddling out to the boat, and therefore I assumed that there must be another method as yet unknown to me.

I had never boarded a boat via a gangway before, but then this was a ship. Boats were small wooden things on boating lakes and until this day in early September, 1958, those were the only boats I knew. The sheer size of this boat was almost unimaginable to me. There was any amount of stairways, passageways, rooms, shops and even cafes. I could not imagine how this huge thing could float, but float it unfortunately did. Not only did it float, but it would travel through the sea at great speed and unknown to me at this time, take me far away from everything I loved and everything that meant anything to me.

I think a feast of chocolate and the excitement of sailing on this huge ship must have masked the purpose of this truly exciting day. As the *S.S. Manxman* pulled clear of Douglas harbour and her engines went full ahead, I recall asking my mother what was the cause of all this bumping and shaking! She informed me that every bump I felt was the ship hitting a fish. I thought, indeed why bother catching a boat if there was that many fish in the sea, we could have walked it. The first moment of truth hit me when we were stood out on deck and I heard my mother say, "I think we are nearly in Liverpool now." I was certainly aware that I was a long way from home and maybe this day was not going to continue with the excitement it had first promised. I vividly recall the industrial smell of the River Mersey as we drew near to Liverpool, although as a five-year-old I would certainly not have attributed this smell to its polluted waters. It was certainly different. Until now, I had only breathed the clean, sweet air and savoured the fresh, invigorating sea that surrounded my Island home.

Disembarkation from the *Manxman* at the Pier Head in Liverpool is only a vague memory, but I recall vividly being struck by the sheer noise, hustle and bustle of Liverpool. At home in Castletown, we had a choice of two buses, the one that went to Douglas and the one that brought you home again. My mother and Auntie Dot now had a choice of probably hundreds. I also only vaguely remember the six-mile bus ride from the Pier Head to West Derby where St Vincent's School for the Blind was, and still is, located. St Vincent's was three schools within one building, the infants, the juniors and the seniors. The kids were all boarders, and from the age of five they would remain at the school until the age of sixteen. In that September of 1958, I started the first of what was to be an eleven-year stint. The idea that I was going to school didn't really hit me until we had walked up the gravelly drive that led to St Vincent's and were stand-

8

ing on the iron grid that lay before the front steps to the convent. I can still recall the sound of the door bell which my mother rang at the school, and hear Sister Allie, the Mother Superior, saying, "Good afternoon, Mrs Glassey. This must be Thomas." This was the first time I had ever been called Thomas, but then it was a first time for lots of things and the slight name change was nothing compared to what was to come.

We, my mother, Auntie Dot and me, climbed the three or four stone steps that led to the highly polished tiled floor of the front porch and stood together with Sister Allie. "Well, we'll take care of Thomas now," she said. My mother's voice was by now breaking into tears. I don't recall hearing Auntie Dot speak at all. A hand had reached out and grabbed mine firmly; it was not my mother's and it had a kind of icy coldness about it. As I heard my mother's footsteps fading away on the gravel drive, the tears started to flow. A hand came down on the back of my wrist and to this day, I can still hear Sister Allie's, "You can stop that nonsense here and now. You're a big boy now and you have started school. We'll soon knock that out of you." Realisation was sinking in that Mum, Dad and Castletown were history. I was in a big strange and horrible place and with Mum now gone, I could do nothing about it and there was no longer anyone around I could turn to for help.

Sister Allie led me into a small room to the left of the main hallway. This was the calming down room. The small wooden-floored room did not seem quite as hostile as the much larger tiled main hallway. I don't know whether my tears eventually came to a stop through the sheer terror of Sister Allie or through simply realising the sheer hopelessness of my situation. "This is a wonderful school and you are a very lucky child to be here," she explained. "Shortly, I will take you from here to where you will be handed over to Sister Mary who runs the infants school." I remember hearing the doorbell ring several times. Every time the bell rang, Sister Allie would leave the room to greet the newly-arriving guests, and after a short welcome I would hear the big doors close, the child's cry and the smack. Sister Allie certainly had a unique method of greeting her guests. I don't know where these new arrivals were taken, but for whatever reason they didn't come in to join me, and Sister Allie always returned to me after going through her arrival ritual. When she announced that it was now time for me to be taken to the infants school, I had recovered my composure somewhat. I think hearing the cries of the other kids and realising that her smacks were not a special treat for me, had played a small part in helping me adjust to this weird and anything but homely environment.

Sister Allie had a vice-like grip on my arm as she led me down the long corridor to the infants school. I had never before walked so far and remained within one building. As we walked along the seemingly endless corridor, Sister Allie explained how I would be expected to find my own way around the school in future and with this in mind she gave a commentary on every room and passageway we passed on our journey. On reaching the infants section of the school, we were duly met by Sister Mary. "This is Thomas," said Sister Allie, "and he is from the Isle of Man." - as if this was significant. She released her grip and with a few parting words which went something like: "Now, Thomas, you are in the care of Sister Mary. She will look after you from now on and any bad behaviour, and that includes any of that silly crying to go home, will be reported to me and so for your sake we had better have none of it." She then chatted to Sister Mary briefly and was gone.

If Sister Allie had come over as a hard and ruthless woman then sister Mary was the complete opposite. Sister Mary was a softly spo-ken, kindly Irish nun. As soon as Sister Allie was out of sight, she took me to the playroom. All my toys had been unpacked and placed in a locker that was to be mine. She introduced me to the two kids who had lockers on either side of me and instructed us to play together, informing us that she would be back later to show us our bedrooms, classrooms and so on. "I will be back to see you all later, and when I return I want to see no more tears from any of you. I know you are all far away from your mums and dads but after a few days with me, none of you will want to go home again." I don't think she actually left the room at all. I'm sure she took advantage of the fact that we kids were blind and she simply wanted us to relax and wind down. It worked, and soon there was not a sob to be heard as we showed off our toys and took the first steps in mate making.

I don't remember my first evening meal at St Vincent's or the guided tour of the classrooms and so on but I'm sure I had both. My last memory of that momentous day is the going-to-bed procedure and procedure it certainly was. Up until now, I had shared the same bed as my younger brother, Kevin. At the end of the day we simply undressed, threw our clothes on the floor and jumped into bed and after a bit of playing around fell asleep and woke up the next day. At St Vincent's, going to bed was to be a much more complicated affair. I would now sleep not in a bedroom, but a dormitory. Instead of sharing a bed, I now had a whole bed, albeit a small bed, to myself but shared the bedroom with about twelve others.

My first lesson at St Vincent's was in the art of going to bed. Sister Mary delivered it according to her usual kind method. She picked up the first few garments I had discarded on the floor and placed them on the bed. "Now Thomas, is this what you have been doing at home?". "Yes, Sister," I replied. "Well there will be no more of that. From now on you will fold everything and place it in your locker." She then introduced me to something I had never heard of before, a coat-like thing she referred to as a dressing gown. This was not the only new item of clothing I was to become accustomed to. There were also things called pyjamas. Changing into my pyjamas, dressing gown and slippers was a very strange experience as all three items of clothing were new to me. However, there was another first on its way. Going to bed now had turned into something of a ritual. No longer would I simply throw off my clothes and jump in to bed. From now on I would change into my pyjamas, wear a dressing gown and slippers, wash and clean my teeth and then say my night-time prayers.

Sister Mary allowed us all to climb into bed before she ordered us all out again. By now she must have been thinking she had inherited a load of five-year-old pagans. She began by teaching each one of us individually the sign of the cross. "In the name of the Father, and of the Son, and of the Holy Ghost." These words were uttered keeping your left hand on your heart and making the sign of the cross with the right hand. It did seem a very weird thing to do as a five-year-old. I certainly didn't understand it but if I thought the sign of the cross was strange, then that was nothing compared to the words of the going-to-bed prayer:

I lay my body down to sleep
and pray to God my soul to keep,
and if I die before I wake,
I pray to God my soul to take.

11

It had never occurred to me that I might die during the night and I remember feeling just a little uneasy about going to sleep. Before leaving us for the night, she paid a visit to each child and explained how we would feel better in the morning whilst tucking each bed in. She announced she was putting out the lights and that there would be no talking from now on; she was sleeping very near and would be able to hear everything. She needn't have bothered saying anything about the talking bit, for dressed in unfamiliar clothes, performing some weird practices and in a strange place I - and I don't think anyone else - was not up to talking. In this strange bed with its perfectly creased sheets and no younger brother sharing it, home seemed a million miles away and soon the tears freely flowed. My only comfort was the sound of sobs coming from just about every other bed. If you can cry yourself to sleep, then I guess that's what happened to me and the other eleven or so infants on that darkest of nights.

Chapter Two

When the "time to wake up, boys" call came at 7.30 the next morning, it was not the voice of Sister Mary we heard but the quiet and gentle voice of Miss Allen. Miss Allen, we were delighted to discover, was not a nun! Although Sister Mary was certainly one of the more endearing sisters, I think we were all very much relieved to learn that we were not going to be in the care of nuns the whole time. Miss Allen was a sort of housemaid and although Sister Mary was very much in charge, Miss Allen would look after many of the day-to-day needs of us infants. The "time to get up" call was the first of the many calls I would now hear for the next eleven years. From now on there would be a time for everything. A time to get up. A time to go to bed. A time for break-fast, a time for lunch. A time to go out, a time to come in. A time for everything. There would even be a time to eat sweets, a time to drink, play and pray. From now on life would be so structured that nothing would take place outside its correct time zone. The "Mum, I'm hun-gry" or, "Can I have a drink of pop" days were history. Nonetheless, I think we were all somewhat relieved to find that at least the first part of the day in this strange place was not in the care of a nun, for nuns, even on a bunch of five-year-olds, had much the same effect as policemen. There was a kind of coldness about the nuns that is not easily explained. I never remember a nun hugging or even touching a child. It was almost as if we had been introduced to another species of the human race.

Getting up on that first morning was a similar experience to that of the night before. There would be no more jumping out of bed and running downstairs. First there was the dressing gown and slippers to put on, then the trip to the washroom. The washroom was a long narrow room at the end of the dormitory. On one side of it were half a dozen wash basins, on the other side, twelve lockers or cubby-holes. Miss Allen guided each one of us individually to the washroom and explained how each basin was allocated between two of us. She taught us to count from the end until we had located our correct basin. The same procedure was applied to the cubby-holes, and although Sister Mary had done all this the previous night, I think that none of us, through fear both of her and of the unknown, had taken a word of it in. Sister Mary was certainly one of the softer of the nuns but compared to an ordinary lady she was tough.

We soon learned that at school there were "ordinary ladies" who were basically the kind of people we were all familiar with, just like people from home. Most of them did not live in at the school and came in on a daily basis, unlike the nuns who rarely left the convent grounds. The "ordinary ladies", as we called them, lived in ordinary houses and were mums and dads themselves. I think this gave them a sharp edge over the nuns on us infants. Miss Allen was one of these "ordinary ladies". Although I have already said that Sister Mary was a quietly-spoken, gentle person, for all that she was still a nun and had a kind of ruthlessness that wasn't normally found in the "ordinary ladies". Miss Allen knew that she could not dress us as our mothers had been accustomed to do at home, for Sister Mary would expect us to be able to dress ourselves when it was her turn to come on duty the next morning. Nevertheless, the tension was somewhat easier getting dressed on that first morning, with Miss Allen in charge. The fear of being smacked, or merely shouted at for getting it wrong, had gone, although Sister Mary never seemed very far away and, God forbid, there was always the threat of Sister Allie putting in an appearance.

Meal times for me, and I think for most of the other kids, were about to change out of all recognition. From now on, breakfast would be at 8 a.m., dinner at 1 p.m. and tea, known at the convent as supper, would be at 5 p.m. Up until now I had eaten everything with a spoon, with my mother cutting up the food first. A knife and fork was thought to be too difficult. From now on, I would have to use a knife and fork. Spoons would only be permitted for eating puddings and even then would be accompanied by a fork. Once again, prayers were said. They preceded each meal and were known as "grace". Up until now God had not really figured much in my life; He was sure going to make up for it good style.

I think what makes the first breakfast stick in my mind is that it was sausages. Sausages are not the easiest of things to cut up with a knife and fork, especially if your only previous experience of eating them was by picking up a sausage with your fingers and slowly reducing it to nothing by a series of bites. As I was about to learn, it took quite a lot to rattle Sister Mary, well at least by a nun's standards, at any rate. However, picking up my sausage and stuffing it into my mouth had an effect on her that could have scarred her for life. I can't remember whether or not I was allowed to finish the first of my two sausages by the method I preferred. The name "Thomas Glassey" rang out through the dining room, then a knife was thrust into my right hand and a fork into my left. With each of my hands in Sister Mary's tight grip, we cut the remaining sausage. "From now on," she retorted, "you will eat all your meals with a knife and fork and you will cut all your own food up as well." She then went on to address the whole dining room. "All meals will be eaten in total silence and when you have finished your meal, no one will leave the table without permission." I was glad to see the back of breakfast and was not looking forward to dinner.

After the first few days had passed, the strange customs of the school became the norm. Although as the crow flies I was about 80 miles from home, the strange environment of the convent, the totally new way of life and the total absence of any members of my family, made it seem as though I was on the other side of the world. The nine until four part of my day that was spent in the classroom didn't seem too bad. My mind was occupied and I enjoyed learning. It was before and after class periods that I had the problem with; too much time to dwell and think, always of home.

My first teacher, Miss Ward, was a kindly soul and I cannot recall a time when she lost her temper or shouted at us. Learning Braille was taking up most of my lesson times in those early days. The equipment for writing Braille was very basic. It consisted of a metal frame across which a piece of paper was stretched, and a metal spike, similar to a nail with a wooden head, which was used to punch holes in

15

the paper forming small dots on the other side. All the Braille text appeared on the other side of the paper, so in order to read what you had written it was necessary to remove the paper from the writing frame and turn the paper over. In 1958 this primitive method of producing Braille was coming to an end and it wasn't long before I was the proud owner of my very own Braille writing machine. I didn't know any kids who owned their own typewriter, so to have my own desk with my own Braille machine made the classroom not a bad place to be.

However, it wasn't just the classroom where all the learning would take place. The school owned its own 50-acre farm and on the boundary of the school grounds was a large woodland. We would have one nature lesson a week and this was nearly always a trip to the woods. On other occasions there would be trips to the school farm. On arrival, we would be given lumps of sugar for the donkeys and clumps of hay or grass to feed the cows. At least once a week, during the evenings, the donkeys would be brought round from the farm to the school to give us kids rides around the school playing fields. In the playground there was a roundabout, a rocking horse and a paddling pool. I think that if it had been a school I was coming in to at nine and going home at four, wild horses wouldn't have kept me away from the place.

My memories of the rest of that first term spent in the infants school are a bit vague. My only contact with home was a weekly phone call from my mother. This would take place every Friday evening at six o'clock. In those days all long distance calls had to be made through the operator. For half a crown, or twelve and a half pence in today's money, she would be allowed a three minute call. At about 5.50 p.m. Sister Mary would arrive to take me down the corridor to the school phone box. She would then open the cubicle door, sit me in the wicker seat, close the door and leave me to wait for the ring. Waiting for the phone to ring was quite a nerve-racking experience. We had no telephone at home and Mother would have to go to the phone box that was just across the road from where we lived. "What if there was someone in the box and she couldn't make the call?" "What if she had no money?" But worst of all, sometimes the phone would ring only for me to find that it was someone else's mother wanting some other child. When this happened Sister Mary would intercept the call and inform the caller that this was not their allotted time and unless it was an emergency they should ring off and call back at the allocated time. When the phone eventually did ring, even the operator's voice instructing Mother to insert two and six and press button B was a welcome blast from home.

The operators in Douglas soon became familiar with my mother's frequent calls and now that they will all be safely retired, I can reveal that they often gave Mother much longer that the three minutes she had paid for. The phone calls were always a sort of setback in as much as I always had a severe attack of homesickness immediately after the calls. These bouts of homesickness were much worse on the occasions when she brought my brothers Lenny and Kevin to the phone with her. Now and again Dad would make the call with her, but he was very much restricted by the shifts he had to work at the Castletown Gas Works. Although my mother's heart was broken by our enforced separation, she seemed to find the strength from somewhere to do whatever was necessary, whereas Dad was like me and struggled to cope with the emotion of it all. Like me, he usually lost the fight against the tears. Sometimes after these phone calls it would be a tearful journey back along the corridor and when this was the case, Sister Mary would inform me that there would be no more phone calls if they were going to be followed by tears.

Apart from the phone calls and the letters from home, the other highlight was the sweet parcels sent from home about once a month or so. Every morning after breakfast, usually in the school playground, Sister Mary would call out every child by name if they had a letter. She would then read the letter to you and hand it over to you. I always kept the letter long after it had been read. Even though I couldn't read the letter, it was something from home and it made me feel better for having it about my person. Even better than the letters was when Sister Mary called out your name and informed you that you had a parcel. The thrill of opening the sweet parcel, all those sweets, even though they would be taken from me and I would be given one bar of chocolate or packet of sweets a day, just seeing all those sweets in one pile just for that brief moment was such a joy.

Chapter Three

Without doubt the most exciting day of the school term was the day that was to become known as "going home day". It was a day that vastly surpassed my birthday, even Christmas Day. I would start looking forward to it several weeks before it came. I can't actually say that my first going home day stands out in my memory. I suppose going home for the first time was not as impacting as the first day at school, but nonetheless, I have never reached such levels of excitement that these special days brought in anything I have done since. I would not sleep very much, if at all, the night before and had no difficulty in getting out of bed when called in the morning. For three months of the school term, I had dressed every day in the school uniform, but on this day I would dress in the clothes of home. My clothes, not the school's clothes. They not only felt different, but they had the smell of home about them. There was a much more relaxed atmosphere about the school and even the breakfast period, normally spent in silence, was filled with chatter. Generally the normal strict rules of the school on this day were overlooked or simply just not applied. The rigidly-strict nuns would give way and be overpowed by the rising tide of children's excitement. On these days there would only be a half school day. School would finish at twelve and once school dinner had been served up (but not often eaten) kids' parents would start turning up at the school, collect their offspring, and head for the railway station.

We would all gather in the front hall and sit and wait for Mum or Dad to arrive. That same front hall which had previously filled me with horror. It was now a place of great joy and if there were any tears, no one was going to be slapped for crying this time. We sat on chairs on each side of the hall and waited. I could hear the sound of the approaching footsteps on the gravelly driveway long before the sound of the doorbell. It was better than waiting for Father Christmas.

My first school holiday was Christmas, 1958. During the winter period the Isle of Man Steam Packet Company operated just the one passage to and from the Island per day. They did this by keeping two of their fleet of about eight vessels in service for the winter period. One left Douglas at 9 a.m. arriving in Liverpool at 1 p.m. The other left Liverpool at 11 a.m., arriving in Douglas at 3 p.m. Because I did not get out of school until 1 p.m. and could not be at the boat before 2 p.m. during winter months, this meant an overnight stay in a hotel in Liverpool. It was always Mother who came over during the winter as Dad would have lost two shifts at the Gas Works and money was very precious and scarce in those days.

The landing stage at Liverpool was a magical place for any kid to be if they were interested in ships or the sea. It was a hive of activity. At the south end of the stage there were the Mersey ferries, coming and going every five minutes or so. The northern end and middle section were taken up by the Isle of Man Steam Packet ships, and by the transatlantic liners belonging to the Canadian and Pacific Railway Company which in the 1950s operated many ships on various routes. In the early 1960s, the C.P.R. line operated two vessels on the Liverpool to Montreal route: the *Empress of Canada* and the *Empress of England*. My beloved Isle of Man Steam Packet ships usually berthed just behind these monsters. As we stood on the landing stage I would be totally transfixed by the noise and activity going on on the landing stage. My first question to my mother would be: "What's the name of the boat?" and she would get no peace until she had divulged this information to me. In my early years at school the Steam Packet operated eight passenger ships. These were in the main passenger-only vessels; however, they did carry a few cars, which had to be craned on board. They also carried mail and a small amount of freight. From the age of five I knew all their names: *Snaefell, Manxman, Tynwald, King Orry, Mona's Queen, Mona's Isle, Ben-my-Chree* and *Lady of Man*. They were all steam-turbine-driven ships and were a focal point at the Pier Head in Liverpool. I simply adored sailing on these vessels - well, at least in one direction, at any rate!

As we edged our way to the foot of the gangway, Mother panicking as she had usually lost or mislaid the tickets, I would be almost bursting with excitement. In Liverpool, the gangway to the Isle of Man steamers was very steep and long, because the landing stage floated, and rose up and down with the tide, so that the distance between the stage and the deck of the vessel was always the same no matter what the state of the tide was. Once I felt the metal beneath my feet and the wood of the hand rail along which I trailed my hand, I was truly on my way home. Stepping on to the deck of the Isle of Man steamer was always special; that magical moment when shoe leather meets wood. There was the distant hiss of the idle steam engines, the smell of rope and the sound of whistling deck hands scurrying about the ship, passengers being directed to the various ship's lounges, newspapers being sold at the top of the gangway and baggage being handed in for safe keeping during the voyage. Often as soon as we boarded the vessel one of the crew would approach us. He would either be from the Castletown area of the Island or just know us for one reason or another. It was music to my ears even from a very early age to hear my first Manx accent for three months. I was now not just merely heading for home but listening to the voice of home, for these people were the tongue of the rock I had been born to love.

I would always make sure that I was out on the deck for the leaving of Liverpool, standing on the landing stage side of the vessel with both hands clasped to the rail. Five minutes before sailing came the blast on the ship's whistle. A truly magical sound. The blast of the whistle always had the desired hurrying effect on people. The activity on the landing stage increased. Chains would now be clinking, heavy steel doors were being closed and bolted and dock workers shouted to each other on the landing stage. The last sound I would hear before leaving the landing stage would be the sound of the chains that held the gangway in place being removed, and then the sound of steel scraping on steel as the gangway was lowered down on to the stage. With the ropes now off and the vibration under my feet, the message was loud and clear - I was on my way home. As the ship gently edged away from the landing stage and pulled out into the river, I could hear the fizzy noise of the water against the ship's side.

20

This would soon change into a much heavier swishy sound as the ship increased her speed. Once we had pulled out into the river, we were now heading for the Irish Sea some 16 miles down river. With the smell of the mucky Mersey in my nostrils and the salty wind blowing in my face, Mother would insist we now went down below to one of the lounges.

There were two sets of stairs leading down to the second class passenger lounges. The first set led to the shelter deck and once there, before we descended to the lounge, we would have to pass the ventilation shaft from the engine room. I would linger here for a moment as I loved the smell, the sound of the engines and the hot steamy atmosphere. Then on we would go, down into the lounge. Downstairs in the second class passenger saloon was about the most boring place a child could be on a ship. The one plus in its favour was that there was more vibration due to us being much nearer to the engines. My mother would instruct me, "Go to sleep and you'll be home before you know it!" Go to sleep! Absolutely no chance! I was on my way home for the first time in three months. I was sailing on a big sea-going ship and going to sleep was definitely not on my agenda. I was going home for about two and a half weeks and I was not going to waste a second of it with unnecessary sleep. Soon Mother would be sleeping but I would be sitting bolt upright, fully absorbing every motion of the ship. On a wild day I was in for a real treat. There would be the sound of the waves thudding against the side of the ship and the creaking of all the ship's fittings as she rolled and pitched her way to Douglas. On days like these, Mother's sleeping would only be broken to be seasick. For me the ship could turn over and I still wouldn't be sick, although when travelling back to school I would often be sick before the ship had even left the quayside. If it was a calm day, the journey would take forever.

In my first three months in school they had taught me how to tell the time and I had acquired a Braille watch. This was the first sign to my family and friends that I had now started school. Everyone thought the watch was marvellous; they would never have seen a Braille watch before and the fact that I could use it was proof that my going away to this far-off special school was working. With my Braille watch, I could tell exactly where we were. After one hour I knew we were leaving the Mersey and crossing the Bar, the point

21

where the river meets the Irish Sea. There would now be an increase in the ship's vibration as she went up to full speed, unrestricted by the river regulations. If the sailing was stormy, once we had left the shelter of the river and were in the open sea the vessel's rolling and pitching would become much more violent; and I would be left to my thoughts for the rest of the journey. On a calm sailing, Mother would wake from time to time and go to buy a mug of tea and a pie for each of us. The pie was just a basic Steam Packet meat pie, but it would taste wonderful, as pies were not part of the institutional food I had been fed on for the last three months at St Vincent's. As Mother chatted to other passengers, some of whom would be from the south of the Island where we lived, my thoughts would race ahead to what I would be doing in a few hours time. There was Bonzo, our springer spaniel dog. Would he remember me? After all, three months was a hell of a long time to be parted. With my two brothers, Lenny and Kevin, I would make straight for the beach. Time passed by so slowly as I day-dreamed the journey home.

When the magical moment came that was signalled by the vibrations of the engines becoming much reduced, I knew that our speed had been cut and we were nearing Douglas. With my suitcase in my hand and mother's bits and pieces gathered up, we made our way up on to the deck. No mucky Mersey smells now, just the sweet salt air of Douglas. No busy traffic noises, just the sound of the gulls. With my ears ringing from the clanking of chains and the rumble of the steel doors being rolled open, I heard the thud of the steel gangway meeting the timber deck. Before long the queue of passengers would start to move forward. As we approached the gangway the hand of a seaman placed my hand on the rail of the gangway a few paces along the metal ramp. One step down and I was on the quay at Douglas. I could have kissed the ground.

As the bus slowly made its way along the nine miles from Douglas to Castletown, I knew every twist and turn. The slow haul up Richmond Hill just outside Douglas, the sharp right turn at the Black Boards corner, the bump of the bus as it crossed the railway lines as it made its way towards Ronaldsway Airport. Then finally, the left turn out of the airport and the next stop was Janet's Corner, Castletown. My stop. I was home, wonderful, wonderful home! My two brothers would always be in the house when I arrived. If Dad did not have a shift at the Gas Works he would be there, too. So would Bonzo, our spaniel. As I entered the house, he would go mad darting round and round the house knocking all kinds of things over, bouncing from chair to chair and finally wrapping his two front paws around my neck and licking my face furiously. Tears of overwhelming joy would once again surface; Bonzo had not forgotten me! I couldn't wait to get to the beach. It would be about four o'clock in the afternoon; and in the wintertime, it would be nearly dark. With Mother's words ringing in our ears, "Be back here in half an hour as soon as it gets dark," we were gone, me, Kev, Lenny and Bonzo, and a few mates picked up along the way.

Chapter Four

Our house, Number 2, King William's Way, was the first house on the Janet's Corner council house estate. Its official name, Janet's Corner, was apparently derived from the name of the lady who once ran the local shop; but it was known locally as "The Camp"- from wartime days. The beach was about 300 yards from our back gate. Within about three or four minutes of leaving home I could hear the sound of Bonzo's paws galloping across the sand, the cry of the curlew and the distant peal of the bell buoy that was positioned about a mile out in Castletown Bay. With all this music in my ears and the feel of the sand beneath my feet, I was once again walking in the sands of home. On the wide open spaces of the beach I could run over large distances without the fear of bumping into obstacles. There were also places such as Langness, the peninsula that forms the boundary between Castletown Bay to the south, and Derbyhaven to the north. Langness provided many riches; plenty of open space and a lush carpet of grassy turf for me to fall on. Its booming fog horn could be heard all over Castletown, and the three lighthouse keepers on station out there always seemed to have time for us kids when we swooped in on one of our unannounced inspections.

During my childhood, Castletown was a small town with a population of less than 2,000 people. Its quiet, narrow streets meant I could wander through the town largely untroubled by traffic. Of course everyone knew who I was and I would often be returned home if I strayed too far. The town's small tidal harbour was another of my favourite places. I would sit for hours and hours on the quayside and be quite content just to listen to the small boats coming and going. Sometimes we would fish with handlines from the wooden swing bridge that spanned the seaward end of the harbour. I don't ever remember actually catching anything, but it was enough just to hear the sound of the boats passing underneath the bridge.

In the early 1960s there was plenty of commercial shipping going on. The Ramsey Steam Ship Company, which operated out of the port of Ramsey in the north of the Island, brought most of the cargoes that came into Castletown. All the names of the Company's ships were prefixed with the word "Ben", the Manx Gaelic meaning "girl". The ships had names such as *Ben Ellan* (Island Girl), *Ben Rean* (Reigning Girl), *Ben Vooar* (Big Girl) and *Ben Veg* (Little Girl). Hence they became known colloquially as "the Ben Boats". They were small steamers and carried about 250 tons of cargo, which normally consisted of coal, cement, salt or gravel. The men who unloaded them were not full-time dockers, for the boats were irregular and couldn't be relied upon for a regular income. Between shifts at the Gas Works, my dad was one of these men. To this day, I have never met any man who worked so physically hard, for so little reward, as my dad. He

A happy threesome. The author, centre, with his brothers Lennie and Kevin, sitting by one of the Ben boats on Castletown quayside.

would frequently start a night shift at 10 p.m., come away at six the following morning, go straight to a waiting "Ben Boat", start unloading at seven, finish at six in the evening and be back at the Gas Works for the following night shift at ten.

In the Gas Works my dad worked as a stoker, a filthy, horrible job

25

Ramsey Steamship Company's 'Ben Ain' seen here at Castletown unloading a cargo of coal. The author was a frequent visitor to the Ben boats, the arrival of which provided his father with an opportunity to earn extra money for the family.

in which few lasted very long. He came to the Gas Works in the mid-'fifties after working on farms and remained there until it closed down in the late 'sixties. The job mainly entailed raking out the retorts of coke and hot ash and then filling them with coal. This was all done by hand, as no mechanical means of carrying out this work ever arrived at Castletown Gas Works. The coke would be raked out of the fires using long-handled steel rakes. When raking out the coke from the back of these ovens, it was necessary to stand right up close to the retorts in order for the rake to grip the coke from the back of the retort. The heat at this point would be just about as much as any man could stand. Once the coke had been raked out and loaded into a wheelbarrow, buckets of hot water would be thrown over the hot coke to cool it down. I often accompanied my dad on one of his night shifts and it was indeed this part of the operation I enjoyed the most. I loved the sound of the hissing, fizzing water as it hit the hot coke. Dad would throw the first bucket which would enable me to judge, by the noise, the direction for the other ten buckets or so, for this job had now been delegated to me. There was more than one occasion whereby I completely misjudged the sound and Dad got a bucket of filthy freezing water over him! The wet coke would be wheeled away and tipped out in the yard, then the barrow would be filled with coal and wheeled in and shovelled into the gas retorts. As a child I spent many a night shift at the Gas Works with my dad and then at six in the morning would ride a bike home. It was probably my brother's bike, as I don't recall ever having one of my own. It was probably deemed an unsuitable gift for a blind child. None the less, at six in the morning with very little traffic about I would ride this bike the mile or so from the Gas Works to my home with Dad running alongside on the pavement.

There would not be too many men capable, after finishing one of these shifts, of stepping straight on to a boat ready, along with five other men, to start at 7 a.m. discharging 250 tons of coal with shovels alone. When Dad had a boat in during my holidays at home, I was in for another treat. Coal boats were discharged in the following way. Six men would go down into the hold of the boat and dig their way through the coal until they hit the bottom of the hold, which was known as the ceiling. This part of the operation was referred to as "digging down" and was often set about in a competitive manner. Needless to say, Dad and his partner, for the six men worked in pairs, usually got down to the ceiling first. The coal was then shovelled into steel tubs, each pair of men having one tub. Once it was full it would be hooked up to a chain or wire rope, and then lifted by a steam winch out of the boat and tipped into waiting wagons on the quay. Once the tub had been emptied, it would be lowered back down into the boat by the same method. The tubs held about five or six cwt of coal and it would be four or five in the evening before the boat was empty. For this Dad and his mates would receive about four quid. It was back-breaking work and there were a couple of die-hards who would make straight for the pub and arrive home with no more money than they had started out with that morning.

At about 9 a.m. the unloading would be brought to a standstill for a tea break. I would always make sure I was down on the quay for this tea break, for Dad would take me aboard the boat so that I could have my tea with the men. There were no gangways to these vessels, they simply lay alongside the harbour wall. If the tide was out, there would be a ladder running from the top of the quay down into the boat. When the tide was fully in, the boat would be about on a level with the top of the quay. Dad would lift me aboard and I would be happy to stand in the galley drinking my mug of tea whilst listening to the

The author, with his father, in the hold of one of the ben boats during the unloading of another cargo of coal.

hiss of the steam winch and feeling the rolling motion of the small steamer as she rubbed up and down on the quayside with the rise and fall of the tide. These boats were always very special to me. I loved the much larger Steam Packet ferries that sailed to and from Liverpool, but they were passenger boats and everyone was allowed on board. On the coal boat berthed in Castletown, the only passenger on board was me. Once the tea break was over, I would be lifted back on to the quay, where I would stay for a while just to listen to the whirl of the steam winch, the sound of the coal being shovelled up from the hold into the tubs and the rumbling noise of the coal being tipped out of the tubs into the wagons. My dad's misfortune to have such physically tiring work was a godsend to me as I loved the dirty, smelly Gas Works, and I simply adored going aboard the "Ben Boats".

Waiting on the quay to take charge of me was Kathleen. From the age of sixteen - ten years my senior - she spent most of her free time looking after my brothers and me, whilst both Dad and Mum were out working. She was an absolute saint, with a heart of gold. Whenever I was home on school holidays, Kath would always be available to take me just about anywhere I wanted to go. She was a young blind child's dream as she seldom said no to anything. She would hold my hand so that I could walk on walls, take me swimming on the beach and say yes to my requests to clamber over the rocks, rather than take the easier route along the roadway into Castletown.

I'm sure that my time spent at home during my school holidays was greatly enriched by my miserable time spent at school, especially during the early years. Having to go to a convent so far away with all its confinements was a bit like plucking a bird from the wild and placing it in a cage. The wild bird has problems in adapting and coping with these restrictions. Then of course, when holidays came around, the cage door was opened and I was like a bird on the wing, as free as the wind and as happy as a king. I suppose you can only appreciate wealth when you have known real poverty, and health when you have suffered illness. When you are taken away from it, home becomes much more than the place where you simply live. All the other kids at school were in the same boat as me. They all had to leave home, they too were parted from their loved ones. Some of them went home for week-ends, but none the less, they were all boarders. However, most of them were from cities around the United Kingdom and I guess they were merely swapping one city for another. They did not share my luxuries of sand and sea and the sheer magic of growing up in such a wonderful place as the Isle of Man. For whatever reason they seemed to cope with the trauma of being separated from their friends and families better than I did.

The last three or four days of the school holidays were always slightly marred by the mounting tension brought on by impending return to school. First there would be the debate between Mother and Father as to which one of them would be taking me. If Dad was on nights at the Gas Works and there was no boat expected for emptying, it would be him, otherwise it would be Mother. On some occasions, after it had been decided that it was to be Dad who would make the crossing, a "Ben Boat" would arrive in Castletown at the last minute and the plan had to be changed back to Mother again. As the dreaded day grew nearer, I would try and cram as many activities as possible into my now very limited time allowance. I would spend as much time on the beach as possible. There would have to be one last walk out to Langness. Would Bonzo remember me the next time I returned? Three months seemed such a long time.

If the last day of the school term rolled by in one big wave of excitement, then the final day of the school holiday was like eating the last of your favourite sweets. I would try hard not to go to sleep on the final night at home, but I guess tiredness and the emotion of what was to happen to me the following day eventually took over and sleep would come. All too soon morning came and I would wake up so damn disappointed that I had not managed to stay awake and drag a few more precious hours from the last night spent in my own bed. Kevin my younger brother slept in the same bed and he would have woken before me. As soon as I woke, he would shed the first of many tears that were going be shed on that day; and once I had heard his tearful break-ing voice the tears would start welling in my eyes. We would both immediately hatch some daft escape plan, which of course couldn't work, but at least it made us both feel better. Mother's call to get up and get dressed would soon follow. We had no central heating and a single coal fire in the living room provided the only heat in the house. Despite this, we never seemed too cold; but on these going-back-to-school days, I was always freezing. I would have no appetite for breakfast, although Mother would point out that in the event of my being sea sick, I should at least have something to come up.

Not a happy boy! The author, smartly dressed in his school uniform, on board one of the Steam Packet ships as he begins another return journey to the dreaded St Vincent's in Liverpool.

The next thing on the check-list was the weather. There was always an outside chance that because of stormy conditions the boat would not be able to sail. But stormy they had to be, for in those days it took an awful lot to stop the Isle of Man boat from sailing. With case packed, and coat on, we would head out to catch the 7.25 a.m.

bus to Douglas. Everyone at the bus stop would know I was going back to school and with a pat on the head and a few coins thrust into my hand they would inevitably finish off with the sentence, "It will be no time at all before you're back again, Tom." They would freely part with their sympathy, which they had in abundance, and also with their money, of which they had very little. The bus would come and we would get on. En route to Douglas, more folks would get on parting with more sympathy and more money. As the bus neared Douglas the welling inside my stomach would now be threatening to rise up and grab me around the throat. It was a short walk from the bus station in Douglas to the pier where the boat was lying, waiting to take the 9 a.m. sailing to Liverpool. Despite my heavy heart, I still got a buzz from stepping on board the Isle of Man steamer. Although, if it was Mother taking me back, it was often because Dad had got a coal boat, or cement boat, in for discharge and therefore was not able to accompany me. Oh how I wished we could swap boats!

I would take up my customary position at the side of the ship with both hands clasped around the rail of the vessel, always making sure I was on the shore side of the boat so that I could hear all the activity on the quay. The first indication that we were moving was when I could hear the sound of the rubber fenders being scraped along the quay wall and the smell of burning rubber. The ship slowly went astern and pulled away from the pier, then backed out into the bay. Soon she would start rolling gently, and the wind would be blowing in my face. This meant we were now turning in the bay. Then came the increase in vibration and with her engines now going full ahead we were on course for Liverpool once again.

As we crossed the Irish Sea my thoughts would drift back to Castletown. What would my brothers be doing now? I could hear the kids shouting and yelling in Victoria Road School, which was only about half a mile from home. I could hear the whirl of the steam winch hauling the coal out of the "Ben Ellan" and the noise of the wagons on the quayside as they made their short journey to Qualtrough's timber yard, just a couple of hundred yards further down the quay. Then the tears would well in my eyes once again as I thought of Bonzo lying mournfully by the back door, not knowing that I had gone far away and would not return for such a long time.

At least Liverpool was four hours away and, after all, I was on a

31

boat, a ship even. Time for a walk out on deck. Some of the crew were from Castletown and trips up to the bridge and a turn on the wheel soon became the norm. One of these Castletown men was Jack Ronan, who lived on the same housing estate as me. Captain Jack, as he became later, was at this time only first officer. He had a son, Billy, and Billy was my buddy, my best mate. If I were fortunate enough to be sailing on Captain Jack's vessel, as soon as he knew we were aboard tea and sandwiches would be sent down to us with one of the stewards. Later another steward would appear to take us up to the bridge. Captain Jack became a great friend and his name will crop up many times in the pages ahead.

The next landmark on the voyage would be at twelve o'clock. This meant we were now three hours into the trip and had crossed the Irish Sea, and the reduction in vibration meant that we had reduced our speed and were now beginning the long crawl up the Mersey. As I sat in the passenger saloon listening to the rest of the passengers chatting amongst themselves, I would really start to feel depressed, as their talk now would be about being able to see land on both sides of the boat. I would always delay gathering up our belongings and going up on deck for as long as I could. Going up on deck at this stage of the crossing was admitting our arrival and by staying down in the passenger saloon for as long as possible meant I hadn't quite arrived yet. Soon enough all the vibrations would cease and the only sound would be the distant hiss of idle steam turbines. Then came the jerk as the ship gently brushed the side of the landing stage. The only noise left to come now was the clinking of the chains that secured the long steep gangway that would take us down to the landing stage. The floating roadway at Liverpool that connected the landing stage to the Pier Head acted as a kind of buffer which masked the real sounds of Liverpool. It was only when you stepped from it and out into the busy flow of the city with its buses, lorries and cars did the noise hit you like a boxing glove. As I clung to Dad's or Mother's arm, I would sense the tension in their movements. They did not move as freely now as they did when guiding me through the quiet sleepy streets of Castletown. They too had to readjust to the much more frantic pace of the big city.

Our arrival time in Liverpool was always at one o'clock, and that never changed, winter and summer. In the summertime my parents would be able to catch the afternoon sailing back at half past three. In winter they would have to spend one night in a Liverpool hotel or go out to St Helens where my Auntie Lizzie lived. Whatever the plan, we would have to find time to go to one of the large department stores to buy a toy to go back to school with. I think this was to soften the blow, but I probably used the situation to apply extra pressure on poor old Dad or Mum to buy a more expensive toy than I would have got, if it hadn't been for the fact that I was going back to school and they probably wouldn't see me again for three months. Money was in very short supply and I often felt very guilty once I was back in the convent knowing that Dad or Mother were wending their way back to the Island, probably without enough cash to buy a cup of tea.

Chapter Five

If my first day at St Vincent's was the worst day of my life, or at least the most traumatic, then the second-worst day was arriving back at school at the age of six and being informed by Sister Mary that I was no longer in the infants. I was going up to the junior school. Sister Mary told me that that I was a big boy now and it was time for me to go and join the other big boys. What made matters worse was not only that I was only six years old and normally infants did not graduate until they were seven, but I was the only child to go up that term. This meant I was leaving all my mates and heading off to the other end of the school. It was a good job I did not know this on the boat or Mother might have had a real job on her hands getting me to come at all. There were more tears as Sister Mary lead me along the corridor. About halfway she stopped and explained to me how much better off I was going to be. For example, I would be allowed to go to bed later and I would be allowed my own wireless, which of course I didn't have. I would be able to go to the school tuck shop. She then informed me that I had got her crying too and that if I didn't tell anyone that she had been crying, she wouldn't tell on me. Of course the tears dried up and when we arrived at the junior school she gave me a hug and parted with the words, "I'll pray for you, Thomas."

The junior school came as a real shock. The kids were all so much older than I was. It was bad enough leaving my brothers and mates behind on the Isle of Man this morning, but to be separated from all my school chums as well was a double blow. My first introduction to the juniors was in the cloakroom. I wandered in and there they all were, jumping up and down and chanting some song or other. I sat down on a bench and waited for them all to disappear, which eventually they did. Once they had all gone I made my way to the toilet area, went into one of the cubicles, bolted the door and wept buckets. Things could not be worse, I missed home. God knows that was hard enough, but now I missed all my infant school mates as well and surely the nun in charge of the junior school would not be as nice as Sister Mary.

My first encounter with Sister Ann was made whilst I was wandering around totally lost somewhere in the school grounds. She explained that she was Sister Ann, and that she was in charge of the juniors. I remember her commenting on the fact that I was very young to be in the juniors and for a brief moment I thought I was going to be returned to the infants. She went on to tell me that Sister Mary had great faith in me, and that although I was a bit young to become a junior I must not let Sister Mary down. Sister Ann did not come over as warm and as kindly as Sister Mary. She spoke with a very stern voice as she explained what would be expected of me. "You will have been taught in the infants how to comb your own hair, tie your shoe laces and do up your own tie. I do not expect to have to waste my time teaching you all these things as you will be familiar with them from the infants. We have better things to do here than teach you things you have already been taught." Well bless my soul, I was in for a rough time as I knew none of these things. Maybe they had not got round to teaching me these things at the infants as they were not expecting me to be moved up to the juniors so soon. However, I was here now and there would certainly not be any allowances made for that. In due course I would learn all these things, but I was severely reprimanded by Sister Ann, not only for not knowing these basic dress matters, but for wasting her time showing me and slowing down the progress of everyone else who, of course, knew these things.

Sister Ann did indeed at first impression seem a very harsh lady, but as time went by she revealed herself to be one of the funniest people I have ever met. I could not imagine that this hard-faced, strict and formal lady would end up displaying a great sense of humour and would be having me laughing myself silly. My first few days in the juniors were spent in constant fear of what might happen to me should I step out of line or not come up to scratch with what was expected of me. These fears were fuelled by the rumours put about by a few of the older juniors. I was informed that the teachers in the senior school carried out all punishments. There were no minor offences it seemed. Just about everything was a hanging offence. Most of the punishments would be carried out by a very awesome head teacher by the name of Mr Fraser. Mr Fraser, so I was informed, had in his classroom a whacking machine. The whacking machine was a small cubicle about the size of a telephone box and inside this machine was a load of sticks that, at the press of a button, whirled around and beat the hell out of you. The seriousness of your crime would determine your length of stay in the whacking machine. "Would you be sent to the whacking machine for not being able to tie your laces?" I tentatively enquired. "Oh yes, you sure will," came the reply. My first three lessons in junior school were learnt in record time. In no time at all I could tie my laces, comb my hair and tie my tie with the best of them. I couldn't wait to tell my infant pals what a hellhole I had been sent too. However the idea that I would see my infant pals again was a wrong assumption on my part, as contact with the infants was strictly forbidden. With hindsight, this was a wise move by the school, for if I had got loose among my infant pals and informed them of what was to be their fate, poor Sister Mary would have had many a sleepless night trying to console crying infants, who would not have been very enthusiastic to leave her loving care.

We were allowed pocket money, but it had to be brought with you at the beginning of term and every penny of it had to be handed over to Sister Ann, not only for safe keeping, but to manage it as well. We were only allowed to spend our pocket money in the school tuck shop and Sister Ann ran that. The shop would open for business every Friday for about half an hour. Firstly you had to go to Sister Ann, who, after carefully studying your finances, would tell you how much you were allowed to spend. In my case it always seemed to be one shilling and eightpence, about seven pence in today's money. When my credit rating looked a bit dodgy, the amount was cut to a shilling and a letter for more funds was quickly drafted and dispatched home. Sister Ann not only dished out the amount of cash you were allowed, but she then slipped behind the counter of the shop and supervised what you bought. Even though she stocked the shop herself, certain sweets, such as gob stoppers, would be banned, so why did she stock them? Well, I think it was a touch of the old Adam and Eve thing, deliver me from temptation and all that stuff. Once the sweets had been purchased, she would promptly swipe them back again and put the lot in a tin. The tin had your name on it and once a day after school had finished, she would open the tin and give you one packet of sweets or a bar of chocolate. Her favourite punishment if you stepped out of line was to ban you from receiving any sweets for that day, sometimes two days, three days depending on the gravity of the offence.

I knew that money was in short supply back home and so it was always with reluctance that I wrote for reinforcements. None the less, a few days later, a letter would turn up from Mother with a Manx ten shilling note enclosed. There was no way Sister Ann was going to accept this 'foreign' money and until she had been to the bank and changed it for English money the only sweets I was going to get were whatever I could cadge. Although the Manx ten bob note was useless to me, I was always a little sorry to have it whipped away and exchanged for the English one, as it was a small fragment of home. It had probably been in my dad's pocket just a few days ago and had been a large percentage of his wages from the Gas Works. The same was true of the sweet parcels I received about once a month. As I counted out all the bars of chocolate, I would imagine the box of goodies sitting on the living room table at home and my two brothers sitting gazing at them, but not touching because they both knew they were for me, far away over the water. They wouldn't have needed to be told by Mother not to touch them, either. I wished that they had helped themselves to at least some of the sweets, I would have felt better. Sweet parcels, letters, money and phone calls from home always brought the tears, something Sister Ann had a big problem in understanding. Still at least I had a home to miss.

I recall an incident that made me take stock and, even at that early age, realise just how fortunate I was to have parents who loved me and friends I cherished. A young girl at the school, we will call her Mary, went down with an illness from which she eventually died. Sister Ann gathered us about her and explained that Mary had died and would be buried here at the school, or at least in the cemetery which was next door to the school. We all attended the girl's funeral and I could not understand why she was not buried at home. I do not recall any of the girl's family being present and for quite some time after this event the thought of dying and being buried in this place, so far away from home, with none of my family at my funeral, haunted me. To add another twist to this sad story we would from time to time be taken on nature walks to visit Mary's grave.

Chapter Six

I recall my first half-term at school vividly. Sister Ann called my name out in the morning post call. She stood in front of me and read the letter from Mother as if she were reading the school rules and regulations. "I'm sorry, Tom, but it simply won't be possible for you to come home this time. Money is very tight and because you don't finish school until one o'clock on Friday there will be no boat until Saturday. You would also have to return to school a day earlier on Monday, in order to have you in for the start of school on Tuesday. This would only give you Saturday afternoon and Sunday at home. I enclose a parcel of sweets and ten shillings and remember you only have six weeks to go and you will be home for the main holidays." I don't have the letter in front of me but I would bet my life I remember it almost word for word. I took the letter from Sister Ann, numb with shock and disbelief. This was the most devastating blow imaginable. I recall burying my head in my locker so that I could not be seen, and weeping buckets. All these bigger and older kids were going home and I wasn't. To hell with Sister Ann and her God who would answer all my prayers, for she had frequently told me that God would look after everything. Well, what the hell was He playing at now? For the only time in my life I had negative thoughts about my beloved Isle of Man. Why was it so far away and so expensive to get to? My faith in God, which had been nurtured by the nuns, was now virtually non-existent. If this was their idea of God, they were welcome to Him. After all, I had done very well without Him before I arrived at this place. In fact my plight had become invariably

39

The 'Royal Daffodil' at the Pier Head, Liverpool. The author spent many happy hours sailing on the ferries which plied across the River Mersey.

worse since they had introduced Him to me. So with no God in my life and no boat ticket in my hand, the coming long week-end looked pretty bleak. However, in the event, it did not turn out to be quite so gloomy.

There was a strange feeling about the morning of half-term. It was only a half-school day and most of the kids would all be gone by lunchtime. Yes, sure I felt sick that I was not going to be at home tonight, but nonetheless, once the kids who were going home had departed, the school became very relaxed. There was just me, four or five Irish kids and maybe one or two from down south. Of course all the nuns remained at the school, but there was only a skeleton staff of domestics such as cleaners and so on. The nuns became much more relaxed and maybe not quite so godly or divine. It may well have just been an impression I had formed, but they didn't seem to pray as much and, of course, they had much more time to spend with the few that were left behind, than they would have had during normal school time. The food became much better, more homely. For instance, things such as chips and beans were now served up. The weekly allowance of pocket money was at least doubled, going to bed was later, we were allowed to talk after lights out and we got up later. The Irish lads and myself would spend most of the night arguing about whose ship was the bigger, my Isle of Man boat, or their Belfast ferry.

Some of the teachers came into school during this period on a purely voluntary basis to take us out into the city and to various places of interest. There were four going-out days, Friday, Saturday, Sunday and Monday. One of these trips out would nearly always be to the pictures. I never did work out why eight or nine blind kids would want to go to the pictures. However a vote was usually taken and I can't imagine the teachers would ever rig such a vote, would they! So pictures it was. Other outings were much more to my liking, such as a trip on the Mersey ferry. From the very earliest days I can remember the sea was an integral part of my life. I loved boats, the waterfront, harbours or just talking to anyone who had anything to do with or knew anything about boats. Having said this, going to the Pier Head, the place my beloved Isle of Man steamers sailed from, was a bit like taking a child to the Christmas grotto only to find when you got there that the real Father Christmas wasn't there and you were not going to get a proper toy from Santa but a bag of sweets instead from a stand-in shop worker. Even so, my first few trips as a young child on the Mersey ferries fuelled my interest in them and as I grew older, I put in many a happy Saturday afternoon sailing back and forth across the Mersey. There would usually be an Isle of Man steamer berthed at the landing stage and as our off-duty teacher would draw this to my attention as we sailed past it, I would get a lump in the throat and would have to hold back the mounting tears which would be welling in my eyes. The thrill of being out on the busy River Mersey, with its big ships coming and going to and from all parts of the world, would soon mask my momentary lapse into home sickness.

Other outings would include visits to the school farm, which, for some reason, we hardly ever visited during school time. There would also be long walks in and around the relatively quiet West Derby suburb of Liverpool. When we were not out on these tours, Sister Ann would take to playing games and spend a lot more time telling us stories of her childhood. I started to like her. From time to time she would make an unscheduled attack on our sweet tins. I almost felt sorry for her as she was departing from her normally strict regime of only dishing out sweets at 4.30 p.m., and felt tempted to hand them back to her.

We still had to attend Mass and so on, even though I was not on very good terms with God at this stage for, as far as I was concerned, He had not answered my prayers regarding going home for half-term. In any case, I don't think I was too keen on getting too involved with God at this stage, as the nuns had not been home for years and after all, they were supposed to be the good ones. Still, the nuns were going to bring us up during our school holidays just as our parents would do if we were home. That was what we were told, so we would go to Mass and say our morning and night prayers and a few more thrown in for good measure. I think the last time my mother and father were in a church was for my christening. As for the morning and night-time prayers, well, if my dad had caught me saying prayers before I went to bed, I think he would have thought that I had got hold of a bottle or two of the Castletown ale that made its way into our house from time to time. My dad was not a religious man; however, he was not anti-religion either. He simply believed that the only rewards he was going to get from life were through hard work, and if prayer had been a possible solution then an awful lot of toil and sweat had been wasted.

On those half-terms when I did get home, which were during the summer periods when there was more than one sailing per day, Dad or Mother would sail over on the 9 a.m. from Douglas, arrive in Liverpool at 1 p.m., take a bus out to the school and have me back aboard the boat for the 3.30 p.m. sailing to Douglas. This would give me Friday night, Saturday, Sunday and Monday at home, with the return to Liverpool on the 9 a.m. boat on Tuesday morning. Mother would write some weeks before the half-term holiday was due telling me that I would be coming home, but I must promise that there would be no tears on my return to school. This was a promise I was happy to give but frequently broke.

Chapter Seven

Another welcome intrusion into the school term were the day trips. These were only possible during the summer periods. Mother or Dad would sail over, sometimes with a friend of the family, on the 9 a.m. sailing from Douglas and return to the Island on the midnight sailing from Liverpool. In Mother's case, she would turn up at the school at about 2 p.m. with a great big bunch of flowers for Sister Allie. This would not meet with my approval. For one thing, in my somewhat juvenile opinion, she did not deserve them, and also it meant there would be less money to spend on our day out. Possibly, Mother was of the misguided view that being nice to our Mother Superior would somehow be reciprocated to me. Mother had much to learn. Sister Allie was totally incorruptible; and I sometimes half-expected my mother to be given a smack for making the gesture. The day out usually consisted of an afternoon spent in the city centre of Liverpool. It meant that I could have a feed of fish and chips, or sausage and beans, rather than the dreadfully boring hard and very dry boiled spuds, meat and cabbage.

If there was enough money there would be a toy. More importantly, I would get the chance to replenish my sweet supply without telling Sister Ann, so that the sweets would not go into my official tin that she kept under lock and key, but to a secret hideaway known only to me and a few mates. Once we had received our allowance of one bar of chocolate or so for the day, which was doled out to us at half past four, my gang and me would skulk off to the hideaway and have a proper feast. From time to time Sister Ann would discover our secret hoard, whereupon it would be immediately seized and given to the poor. Whether she actually parcelled up the sweets and sent them off to Africa, or simply despatched them to some orphans home in Liverpool, we never actually found out. As seven- and eight-year olds, we did wonder what the poor starving folks of the Third World would make of Sister Ann's food parcels of Mars bars, fruit gums and so on. We decided that we were actually doing these poor people a greater favour by hiding away our sweets and forbidden goods, than by our prayers, which we were frequently asked to offer by Sister Ann.

I vividly recall one of these day trips made with my dad. We had spent the afternoon sailing to and fro on the Mersey ferry. On the way back to the school we called into a record shop to buy a record I had wanted which was number one or thereabouts. The song was called "Walking back to Happiness" and was sung by Helen Shapiro. Dad bought the record and then handed it over to me. I held the record in my hands for a while and then gave it back to Dad: "I'm sorry, Dad, but I can't take this where I'm going, for it is you that is walking back to happiness and not me." He took the record from me, as I recall, without comment; and I very much doubt if he ever had the heart to play it on his return home. On that same day out I remember arriving back at school and, to try and draw out the time for as long as possible, dragging Dad off to the school farm. We wandered around the farmyard and then on the way back to that ever-daunting front hallway we sat down on the grass verge. With the tears once again welling in my eyes, Dad pulled from his pocket what seemed to be a huge amount of threepenny bits and sixpences. He told me they were lucky coins and I was to take them for they would bring me luck. I didn't know at that time, but he had literally given me every penny he possessed and after leaving me at the school at about 6 o'clock he now would have to spend until midnight wandering around Liverpool with no money. When he finally boarded the Isle of Man boat, he could not even afford a cup of tea throughout the voyage.

Often after completing one of these day trips Dad would have to go straight from the ferry to the Gas Works to take the next shift. In those days, the pay was very poor indeed for a stoker at the Gas Works, and so one or two of the men would use their initiative, for want of a better word, to supplement their income. This could be done by taking the odd bag of coal or coke; or, if you wanted to help a mate whom you knew was on call, by arranging a call out. The call out method used at our house for attracting Dad's attention was for whoever it was that was calling him out to stand in the road outside the house, frantically throwing stones up at the bedroom window in a bid to wake him. On one such occasion, one of the duty stokers, a lad named Kenny, a likeable sort of rogue, took it upon himself to boost Dad's income and do his bit to help with boat fares and so on. Just as Dad had fallen asleep after coming off the previous night shift, stones started to pelt the windows. Eventually, he rose from his bed and went downstairs to find Kenny at the door with an urgent request for him to return to the Gas Works. "Well, everything was fine when I left it," said Dad. "Well it's not now," retorted Kenny." "I'll have a cup of tea and I'll be down shortly then." "Never mind the tea, this is megga urgent," says Kenny. Without further ado, Dad was thrust into Kenny's car and driven the mile or so to the Gas Works. On his arrival he found the kettle on and simmering away nicely and everything working perfectly. "Well, what's the problem? Everything seems to be fine to me!" Kenny poured the tea mumbling something like, "Four hours overtime won't go amiss, will it?"

Chapter Eight

Sister Ann was a very high flyer where food was concerned. Not only was she in charge of our sweet tins, but she was the breakfast lady, the dinner lady and the evening meal lady. If I ever failed to finish what was on my plate, I would be reminded of the starving people in Africa. I sometimes wondered why, as they had at least half of my sweets! I only wished she would be as generous towards them with my unwanted cabbage and sprouts. I would struggle desperately to wade my way through the seeming mountains of cabbage, sprouts or cauliflower. Just as I was slowly munching my way through the last painful mouthful of the stuff, she would present herself behind my chair banging her ladle up and down in her vegetable dish with her familiar call: "Lovely fresh vegetables for the kiddies, lovely fresh vegetables for Thomas!" I would sit in total despair as another ruddy great heap of cabbage was shovelled onto my plate. With regard to my unwanted large mounds of cabbage and sprouts, help was on its way from an unlikely source. God and I had not exactly seen eye to eye so far, but things were about to change, although the eventual outcome was not exactly the result I had planned.

It was nearing the time for me to make my first confession and take Holy Communion. In the Catholic Church they believed, and as far as I know they still do, that before you can enter the Kingdom of Heaven your soul must be cleansed of sin, and that these sins can only be cleansed by going to the priest with an act of confession. The priest would then grant you absolution and after you had fulfilled the

WHO'S AFRAID OF THE DARK?

penance he gave you, which was usually a load of prayers, if you died before you committed the next sin you could go straight to Heaven. The sacrament of communion meant I could receive the body of Christ in the form of bread during the Mass. I made my first confession when I was eight years old and had my first communion the following day. Making your first communion was a very special day. The kids who were taking part would be given a day off from lessons and were given presents such as boxes of chocolates and so on.

At eight years old I was not too happy about this confession lark. The chances of my dying without any sin on my soul were pretty remote, I figured, and in any case I wasn't too sure that I wanted to go to Heaven anyway. According to what I had been told, certainly Mum and Dad, and for that matter my brothers, wouldn't be there, as they never even went to church. In fact none of my family or friends from home would be there. The only folks who would be there would be all these nuns, priests and teachers from school. No, I would be quite happy down in Hell with Dad and the like. It would be a much better place and it didn't seem too difficult to get there either. All I had to do was die with a enough sins on my soul not to be allowed into Heaven, and in this place I would have plenty of opportunity for sin. I did keep these early observations to myself, however; even at the age of eight it was anything for an easy life.

Now that I was a fully-fledged member of the Catholic Church, I was invited to make the once-a-year sacrifice during the forty-day period of Lent. I was determined to make not one sacrifice but three, and I certainly did not feel hard-done-by when I went to Sister Ann and told her I was giving up cabbage, sprouts and cauliflower for Lent. I was afraid she had rumbled me but it appeared not. I had forty wonderful cabbage- and sprout-free days. It was even better than I could have imagined when, during meal times, I could hear her approach the table with her ruddy great ladle, saying, "No lovely vegetables for Thomas!" It was music I was hearing. However I did not endear myself to those of my mates who also hated the stuff. They received even larger helpings while I made my unselfish sacrifice. Well, they say there's no such thing as a free lunch and I can vouch for that at St Vincent's. There was certainly no such thing as a cabbage-free zone. As we neared the end of Lent, talk would be rife amongst us as to what gifts we would be receiving for keeping up our

sacrifices. Those who had given up sweets would be given sweets galore for being such good children: and yes, I was given endless amounts of cabbage, sprouts and cauliflower. Even when it was carrots or peas for everyone else it was cabbage or sprouts for me. I did not make this mistake again.

I was really only a Catholic whilst attending St Vincent's. At home Mother did not practice the faith, Dad was not a church person and my two brothers both went to a non-denominational school. I would not go as far as to say the nuns were actually hostile towards other religions, but they certainly built firm barriers around themselves, in as much as they saw very little of the outside world and kept us kids away from anything that might have influenced us. A typical example of this was the junior school playing field. A small beck or stream formed the boundary of this field. A high fence had been erected on our side of the bank, although in fairness this was probably to prevent us from falling in the beck more than anything else. However, on the other side of the beck there was some waste ground frequently used as a play area by the kids of West Derby. We were strictly forbidden to talk to these kids for no other reason than that they were Protestants. As far as I was concerned, this made them a very interesting group of kids to talk to, as I tried frantically to discover what was wrong with them. My acquaintance with my new non-Catholic friends frequently got me sent for by Sister Allie but I don't actually remember being punished for it. Just a good talking to and several threats of action were deemed to be enough. Even when I informed my friends from across the stream that when they died they would not be going to Heaven, they showed no urgency to cross the stream and become one of us good guys. I remember telling one of them that Sister Allie had forbidden me to talk to him. He said he would tell his mam and his mam would write to Sister Allie. Every morning for a week, I lived in fear in case my name was read out in the school assembly with regard to the letter she had received. I do not know whether she ever received such a letter. If she did, then she kept it to herself. She may even have replied to it and who knows now, some forty years on, they may well be long-established pen pals.

(Facing page) The author, left, with his schoolmates on Confirmation Day at St Vincent's.

Chapter Nine

A t the end of every summer term the school went on its annual outing. This was a day out for the entire school, infants, junior and seniors; all 120 of us or thereabouts. It was always to the seaside resort of New Brighton. Well, strictly speaking, the Merseyside resort. In the 1960s, with its three fairgrounds (one of which was completely indoors), this resort was a kid's paradise. We were all taken in cars driven and donated for the day by volunteers from the Liverpool area. They were, and as far as I know, still are, a magnificent band of people who gave up their cars and time to take us blind kids out for the day. For this day all three fairgrounds would be closed to the public and given over for the exclusive use of the school. All rides were free of charge. As juniors, there were certain rides that Sister Ann strictly forbade us from going on. One of these was the notorious big wheel. I can still feel the clip round the back of my neck and her voice bellowing in my ear as I took my place in the queue for my turn on the forbidden wheel. At the end of the day, we were all given a carrier bag full of sweets, which was exempt from handing over to Sister Ann. That was fine while the sweets lasted, the only down side was that she appeared to think they were everlasting sweets. For days after she would not open up our sweet cupboard on the grounds that we still had our New Brighton bags. When the fairground closed down around the mid-60s the entertainment was swapped for a cruise aboard the river cruiser, *Royal Iris*. She was a 1300-ton, twin-screwed motor vessel complete with dance floor, coffee bar and plenty of open deck space. The cruise would be

An impressive view of the 'Empress of Canada' cargo/passenger liner which was operated out of Liverpool by the Canadian Pacific Railway.   (Photo: Sea Breezes)

A busy scene at the Prince's Landing Stage, Liverpool showing the Steam Packet's
first car ferry which came into service in 1962   (Photo: Sea Breezes)

to the Mersey Bar and back, and of course I always got a lump in my throat as the little ship turned about for what they called home. It did occur to me to try a little bribe or two on the captain, to persuade him to carry on, but somehow I think it might have taken more than a stick of New Brighton rock to do the trick.

In 1962 I almost got my wish to cross the Atlantic on the *Empress of Canada*. In that same year, the Isle of Man Steam Packet Company launched their new and first car ferry, *Manx Maid*. At the end of term I wanted the *Manx Maid* to be the ship that was to take me home, as my teachers had read all about her to me from reports in the newspapers. I was delighted on going-home day when Mother turned up at the school having crossed over from the Island on the 9 a.m. sailing from Douglas and informed me that we would indeed be sailing home that afternoon on the *Manx Maid*. We took the 12A bus to the Pier Head, and as we stood on the Prince's Landing Stage my mother gasped in amazement at the sheer size of our new ship. "I really don't know how it is going to get into Douglas," she commented. That in its self was quite amazing, as she had crossed over on the new ship from Douglas that very morning. However, we proceeded up the gangway only to be stopped at the top and asked politely as to where we were heading for. "Douglas, of course," said Mother, almost shoving the poor guy out of the way, and implying he must be a bit thick for asking such a question. "Not on this vessel," came the reply. "This is the *Empress of Canada* bound for Montreal!" We trudged back down the gangway, walked along the landing stage and boarded the waiting *Manx Maid* lying just astern of the big liner. My mother's navigational skills were again found wanting just four hours after the *Empress of Canada* saga, as, arrived in Douglas, we headed off to the opposite end of the Island on the wrong bus!

In 1964 I was eleven and home was becoming an even more exciting place to be. I was still doing my shift at the Gas Works and visiting the "Ben Boats" when they were in Castletown. However, many of my holidays were now spent on the sea as a guest of the many boatmen of Castletown. My first trips were on the small 18-foot yacht, *Dorothy M,* which was owned by a close friend of my family, Mr George Squires. His boat was named after his wife, who was the aunt I referred to earlier who had accompanied Mother and me on that first day at St Vincent's. Most of the time we sailed using the Seagull outboard engine. I just adored the motion of a small boat on the sea. At first there was the stillness of the harbour. Then the gentle rise and fall of the boat as she first came into contact with the small waves at the entrance of the harbour. Then, as we hit the open sea, the freshening of the wind on my face and the thud of the larger waves thumping against the bow as the boat sliced her way though the water. I had not simply heard the call of the sea, it was a fixation, an addiction that has stayed with me for life.

Another family friend was Michael Quine, who also owned a small boat. Michael had spent some time working deep sea, mostly on the tankers. However, he was now back in Castletown and was stoking at the Gas Works with Dad. He lived on Janet's Corner just a few doors down from us. I recall an incident that took place on the morning of one of my returning-to-school days. In those days, all the electricity on the Janet's Corner housing estate was fed into the houses through a money-box meter. A shilling would normally give you a couple of hours of electricity. My mother had discovered that if you filed a penny down to the same size as a shilling you could pass the penny off as a shilling. Well, at least as far as the meter was concerned you could. Of course, when the man came to empty the meter and all the pennies were rejected, poor old Dad suddenly had to find a lot of shillings. My mother often spent much time filing down a penny on the back step in order to cook the evening meal, for the gas meter also worked by the same method. I recall hearing Michael's voice one winter's morning as I was getting ready to go to Douglas to catch the 9 a.m. sailing for Liverpool. He had called round to see if we had a shilling for the meter. His baby daughter, Catherine, had taken sick during the night and now, with the electricity running out on him, the situation was obviously becoming grave. I learned later that week that young Catherine died of meningitis shortly afterwards.

Chapter Ten

O n my return to school in September of 1964 I was eleven years old and it was time for me to leave the junior school and head for the seniors. This was not nearly as traumatic as the transition from infants to junior. I knew that I would be going up to senior school and in fact, I was looking forward to it. The seniors had more privileges such as going to bed later, a much bigger play ground, no school tuck shop for I could buy my own sweets now, more or less whenever I wanted them, providing I had the money, of course. My new house sister was to be Sister Cissy, but I would still take the odd trek down the corridor to have word or two with my now good friend, Sister Ann. After spending five years under Sister Ann's wing, I felt that I could cope with anything that anyone could throw at me.

There was also another change afoot. Sister Allie was to move away to another convent, although it might have been retirement - that's if nuns actually do retire. She was to be replaced by Sister Claire. Although most of us lived in fear of Sister Allie, I never actually remember her hitting anybody, apart from on my first day. She just had a sort of awesome presence. Sister Claire was much younger than Sister Allie and although she could be hard when she needed to, generally speaking she was much more approachable than the older nun. Sister Allie was really someone from the 1940s who just never quite caught up with the 1960s.

Up until now, I had been something like a caged bird confined to the convent. I had been crossing the Irish Sea between Douglas and

Liverpool for six years and had built up firm relationships with the crews of the Isle of Man Steam Packet ships. One of these men I referred to earlier, was Captain Jack Ronan. By now, Captain Jack was making regular visits to the school. I would never know when he was going to turn up, but I was always thrilled to bits when class finished at four o'clock and the duty house sister, Sister Cissy, would inform me that I had a visitor. Of course, I would know it was Captain Jack. Well, it had to be, as there was no one else who could visit me during the evening and not need a hotel to sleep in for the night. First, though, Sister Cissy would have to give me permission to leave the convent, and set the time that I was required to return. Once this had been sought and granted, I would be away, although I often got frustrated by not being able to find her and would be counting the precious minutes I was losing. On occasions when I couldn't find her, I would leave word with one of the other pupils; but if they forgot to tell her, it wasn't just me who would be on the wrong end of Sister Cissy's tongue later that night, but Captain Jack as well!

I recall my first outing with Captain Jack. Having made our way up the long gangway to the *Mona's Isle*, I sensed as we stepped on board how much larger the ship seemed now that she was empty. She had sailed over from Douglas at 9 a.m. that morning and now would lie at the landing stage until 11 a.m. the following day. Captain Jack promised me that he would always give me a blast on the ship's whistle at five to eleven just before she sailed. The school was five or six miles away and occasionally I managed to kid myself that I had actually heard it. The first trip set the pattern; after a full tour of the ship, which would include a trip down to the engine room conducted by the ship's chief engineer, whom Captain Jack would think nothing of arousing, we would make for the bridge and enter the wheelhouse. Captain Jack knew I had a fascination with radio and would make a totally bogus call, claiming to be testing the system to Mersey Radio. The only thing he stopped short of was ordering the crew to stand by and take the ship for a short cruise up the river and back. Next, it was time to hit the buffet bar. The good Captain would fill a carrier bag full of sweets right up to the top and once, when I suggested that the chief steward might have something to say tomorrow when he checked his stock, the Captain's reply was: "Well, yes, of course he will notice, but the last person he will suspect is me!"

Family friend, Captain Jack Ronan, who made frequent visits to St Vincent's from where the author was taken to visit Steam Packet vessels laid up for the winter at Morpeth Dock, Birkenhead.

Of the seven or eight vessels that the Steam Packet operated at that time, only two would be in service during the winter period. The rest would be laid up across the river in Birkenhead. When Captain Jack was transferred to one of these ships, it did not deter him from making his way out to St Vincent's to collect me for another of his fascinating tours. These would have to take place at week-ends because of the travel time that would now be involved. Even so, on many a winter's Sunday, Captain Jack would make his way out to St Vincent's and take me out for the afternoon to Morpeth Dock, which was where the Steam Packet ships were laid up for the winter. My journey to his ship was a little bit more interesting than usual, as there was the ferry trip across the Mersey after leaving the bus at the Pier Head. Morpeth Dock was only a short walk from the ferry terminal at Birkenhead. It was not an active dock in as much as there were no ships being discharged or loaded there. It was purely and simply a place for vessels that were surplus to requirements to hibernate. As we made our way along the dockside, the only sound to be heard was the wind blowing through the empty and disused warehouses and the occasional clanking of the odd diesel train as it slowly chugged its way through the dock network, to where, I never knew.

Going on board a laid-up ship was a totally different experience from going aboard in Douglas or at the landing stage at Liverpool. With no passengers and only three or four of a crew which normally numbered about sixty, and with absolutely no background noise whatsoever from engines or any other systems, the ship almost had a eeriness about it. It was difficult to imagine the same vessel just two or three months earlier, thronging with passengers, with kippers and newspapers being sold at the top of the gangway, tea and snacks available from snack bars around the decks and three course meals being served in the dining saloon.

On a winter's Sunday afternoon in Morpeth Dock, Captain Jack and I did not have just one ship to ourselves, more like the whole damn fleet. I would still go for my umpteenth tour of the ship, which was something I never tired of. Then we would sit in Captain Jack's cabin and he, being from my home town of Castletown, would tell me all the news from home. I remember once standing on the bridge of the *Snaefell*, the car ferry *Manx Maid* berthed just opposite us. Captain Jack threw a cork at the *Manx Maid* so that I could get an

The Steam Packet's vessels, 'Manx Maid' and 'Manxman', laid up at Morpeth Dock, Birkenhead, for the winter 'hibernation'.

idea of how far apart the two ships were. I recall saying to him, "Why don't you lob something heavy like a spanner at her porthole, that would tell me how far apart we are, and in this deserted place no one would ever know it was us." "Well, yes," he replied, "but it wouldn't be very manly, would it?" I guess that proved it wasn't just the nuns at St Vincent's who were in sole charge of my education. At around six o'clock, we would wend our way back to St Vincent's. Captain Jack would always give me the choice of whether we crossed the river by ferry or go by train under the Mersey; the train, needless to say, never got my vote. As we crossed the river Captain Jack would provide me with a running commentary on all the activity going on in the river. As we walked up the gravel school drive I always got that despairing feeling, whether I was with Captain Jack, Dad or Mother; how I wished I could swap their lives for mine.

I have much to be grateful for from Captain Jack Ronan. He often gave up his free time when his ships were in Liverpool - sometimes several hours of it. It was a time-consuming exercise for him to come out all the way to West Derby from the dockside in Liverpool, to give a child who wasn't even his responsibility a day out. Much of my early knowledge of the sea came from Captain Jack. I recall being on a cruise on the Mersey aboard the *Royal Iris* when I was about thirteen. The captain had invited us kids from St Vincent's up on to the bridge and after showing us around his wheelhouse, he asked if we had any questions. I can recall the stunned silence from the captain himself and from my teacher as I asked, "Why has your vessel only got a class two passenger carrying certificate?" Captain Jack had explained all these things to me and I was not going to lose the opportunity to put my acquired knowledge to the test. A few weeks later we all stood in the school drive waiting to board a bus to take us on some outing or other. Our teacher was going through all the does and don't, then, just before we boarded the bus, he turned to me and said, "Now then, young Glassey, I do not expect you to ask the driver if you can examine his driving licence."

Captain Jack had more to offer than just the odd Sunday afternoon out. At holiday time, and providing his ship was sailing to Liverpool on the day the school broke up, he would pick me up from the school, saving Dad or Mother the time-consuming two-day journey during the winter. When this happened, I did not have an overnight stay in a

Liverpool hotel but would sleep aboard the boat. This was a big improvement over staying in the hotel. I wasn't exactly home on that first night of the holiday, but I wasn't at school either. I could absorb all the excitement of the busy River Mersey and still have one foot back home. I was surrounded by Manx people, the crew of the ship, all speaking of home and of places I knew and had missed so much over the last three months. During the evening Captain Jack would take me ashore and walk up and down the landing stage explaining all about any other vessels that were alongside that evening. I would then have my supper with Captain Jack and the other officers aboard.

I slept in Captain Jack's cabin, which was on the bridge just behind the wheelhouse. Up until about midnight I would stay awake listening to the Mersey ferries as they made their way across the river. They would have to sail the whole length of our vessel as they cleared the landing stage. Lying in bed at night and listening to the sound of the wash of the ferries and other small river launches sailing past was pure magic to me, and together with the excitement of sailing home on the morrow meant that sleep did not come easily. The following morning, breakfast was delivered to our cabin. Well, I guess that's how captains are treated and if I was in Captain Jack's cabin, then I would be afforded the same respect as he was. At 11 a.m., when the ship pulled away from the landing stage, I would sit in the wheelhouse totally fascinated by all that was going on. "Hard astern, hard to starboard," and so on. I would listen to the ship's radio as Mersey Radio passed instructions to us all the way down the river until we reached the open sea. Then it was home all the way, flat out for Douglas, with an ever-narrowing expanse of water between wonderful home and me. Going home was always special, no matter who was taking me - Captain Jack, Dad, Mother or whoever. The only time my guide mattered was when I was returning to school; for that I wanted no one but Dad or Mother.

Chapter Eleven

E very minute at home was precious. I did not want to lose a single second of the time spent away from school. While on holiday, I still had to get in a couple of night shifts at the Gas Works; but by now Dad had taken to milking Alfie Kenaugh's cows in the morning after he had finished work. Alfie had a small farm just outside Castletown, at Red Gap. Of course, this would have to be added to my list of activities. Alfie looked on Dad's milking as a sort of neighbourly favour; but he always paid me half a crown for my part in the venture. With my night's stoking completed, and the cows milked at Red Gap, it was time to ride my bike home, on the road with Dad trying desperately to keep up with me and maintain control of the bike. We would have to stop off in Castletown at Peggy Watterson's toy shop, as the half crown (about 12 pence in today's money) would be burning a hole in my pocket. As Peggy rummaged through boxes and boxes for a toy boat, I once recall her saying to Dad, in her broad Manx accent, "My God, Dennis, young Tom is as black as a rook, you'd swear he'd been an' dun a shift down at the Gas Works with ya." "He has," said Dad. However, I doubt if she actually believed him.

From time to time, the Manx Blind Welfare Society would send their welfare officer out to visit us. These visits were to keep a check on my rehabilitation as a blind child and to find out how Mother and Dad were coping. We had no phone in those days, so in the main these visits would be unannounced. My mother recalls this incident. "So, where is young Thomas?" enquired Mrs Jones, the Blind Welfare officer. "He's upstairs in bed," says Mother. "Well, what is he doing in bed in the middle of the day at a time when he should be out playing with other children?" Mrs Jones, I guess, was now thinking I had been shoved off to bed out of the way and was obviously rather taken aback by her discovery. "He is in bed because he has been stoking with his dad at the Gas Works all night, and from there he went milking cows." Mrs Jones left saying she would return at a later date. She may well have done and if she did, I was probably assisting Dad on a coal boat or something. One way or another, I'm sure she went away convinced that my rehabilitation was clearly heading in several directions she hadn't bargained for.

The staff of Castletown Gas Works photographed on Sunday, 4th May, 1969, the day when gas production ceased after 115 years. Left to right: Works Manager Walter Cole, Lennie Glassey, Teddy Brew, Sid Faragher, John Squires, Jack Wooler and Dennis Glassey, the author's father.

Dad was one of the few people who very rarely said no to me as a child. He needed no expert training in how to look after a disabled child. The disabilities simply melted away in his presence. "Yes, you can ride a bike, you can stoke, you can milk a cow, you can do everything I do with me." And who was going to argue? By now, I had acquired a bike of my own from somewhere and was riding solo, up and down the pavement outside our house at Janet's Corner. I had worked out how many pedals it took to get from the main road at the entrance of the estate to where the pavement ended at the back of the first row of houses. I would break usually just in time to prevent myself from flying off the end of the pavement, across the road and over the garden wall of the house opposite. During my school holidays the residents of Janet's Corner walked around the estate at great personal risk to themselves. At any time a blind child could come hurtling around the corner on a bike, with no warning bell and without so much as an apology for whistling past them with less than an inch to spare.

I didn't work every shift at the Gas Works with Dad as it was only the night ones that really interested me. There was always something magical about the night period. There was never anyone else about for a start, which always made it a bit special. I suppose being at the Gas Works on the night shift was a bit like being on the Steam Packet boat when there were no passengers on board - you felt sort of privileged. When Dad was on day shifts and there was no one available to look after me at home, I would accompany my mother to her place of work. Mother worked as a cleaner at King William's College. The College was, and still is, a minor public school situated on the outskirts of Castletown. I always got a buzz walking through the College grounds on my way to work with Mother. Well, I guess I would, as I was entering a boarding school and all these kids were stuck here and, unlike them, tonight I would be going home for my tea. I thought they would envy me, but I doubt it. I guess the main difference between my school situation and theirs was that they were all there because either they, or their parents, wanted them to be. Not like me, stuck in a far-away school simply because there was nowhere else to go.

Unlike the Gas Works, cleaning King Bill's did not really appeal to me, so I sought my own entertainment. This usually took the form of pretending the whole College was a ship. On one of these fantasies, I found myself playing in one of the numerous rooms while Mother was cleaning elsewhere in the building. Whilst carrying out a survey of the room I stumbled across a polisher. This was similar to a vacuum cleaner, only instead of sucking it polished. It had two brushes underneath that spun round when it was switched on. This made it an ideal imaginary outboard engine. So with my polisher plugged in and switched on, I started my engine. I discovered that by lifting the brushes off the floor and turning the polisher on its side, the revs would increase dramatically. This meant I was now clear of the harbour and I opened up my outboard engine to the full amount. I was now at sea in my small boat and as happy as a sandpiper until, that is, my polisher suddenly died and I was stranded at sea with a broken engine. The enquiry which included my mother took place around me. They were not too chuffed about having a burnt-out polisher, but there was not a mention of my fate, stuck seven miles off Langness Point with a broken outboard engine!

When I wasn't at the Gas Works, or on a coal boat or with Mother at King Bill's, I could be found playing football with my Janet's Corner mates. Our home ground was a bit of wasteland just across the road from our house. I was the goalkeeper as that was deemed by my team-mates to be the most suitable position for me. I guess their thinking went something along the lines that if you were blind then you should be allowed to use your hands. This wasn't much of a concession, really, as all goalkeepers can use their hands. However, it was one I accepted gratefully. Matches were placed inside the ball so that I could follow it by the sound; only one ball actually exploded. Later, we substituted the matches with tiny ball bearings. We often made the claim that our defence was the best on the Island, but then any defence playing in front of a blind goalkeeper would soon learn that mistakes could prove expensive. We couldn't really lose as, when we won, we were brilliant - and with a blind goalkeeper. When we lost, it was a case of "Well, what do you expect with a blind goalkeeper?"

On Saturday afternoons we would head for Castletown Stadium, the home of Castletown Football Club. I would sit in the tiny stand along with my 40 or 50 commentators, which was about the average attendance in those days, unless we were playing a real crunch match against Peel, or the local derby against Rushen United. One of our supporters, who never missed a game, was and still is Mr Juan Kermode, better known as Hicky. We could hear his voice booming out from the stadium long before we reached the ground. To this day, some 40 years on, Hicky is still there cheering the team on. Even though I no longer attend the matches, as I walk my dog around

Poulson Park on a Saturday afternoon, I can still hear Hicky's voice with his now famous and familiar phrase "Come on the Town!" At that time, a local newspaper, the *Green Final*, containing all the football scores, came out at about six o'clock on a Saturday. When I went back to school my younger brother, Kevin, would send me this newspaper so that I could keep in touch with my team. Many a time my *Green Final* was found blowing around the school playground along with the *Liverpool Echo*, ensuring that names such as Sid Butler, Dennis Moore and Joe Ennet, all of whom played for Castletown at that time, were mentioned by teachers and staff in the same breath as the great Liverpool and Everton players such as Ray Wilson, Alan Ball, Chris Lawler and so on.

It wasn't just the football that kept me busy during the school holidays. There was also the fishing. We fished from the rocks, or occasionally from a boat if we were lucky enough to meet up with someone who was going to sea at the same time as we were mucking about around the harbour area. Most of the time we fished with handlines from the swing bridge that spans the lower part of Castletown harbour. Castletown has a tidal harbour that completely dries out at low water. I recall one occasion when I had nagged my mates so much about going fishing when they obviously didn't want to that, in order to shut me up, they set me up with my hand-line on the swing bridge. With my hook bated and my mates promising that they would be back for me later, I happily spent the next couple of hours waiting for a fish to bite. As far as I am aware I am still the only angler who has spent an afternoon fishing in Castletown harbour with the tide completely out!

Most of my relations lived in Ballasalla and often my younger brother, Kevin, and I would trudge the two mile stretch along the banks of the Silverburn river from Castletown to Ballasalla. I loved the walk along the Silverburn. As a child I could roam freely without the fear of bumping into objects. The grassy banks of the river, and the fields that sprawled out between Castletown and Ballasalla, meant that I had a fitted carpet to land on with every trip along the way. At the age of twelve I could recognise the sound of the raven and the pheasant. These were sounds I did not hear in Liverpool and they gave the place that little extra touch of magic that no country walk could conjure up at school. A waterfall marks the halfway point of the

One of the familiar sounds enjoyed by the author, as he walked along the banks of the Silverburn river to visit relatives at Ballasalla, was that of the steam railway travelling to and from Castletown.

walk. I would pick up the sound of the rushing water several hundred yards before we drew level with it. As we reached it, its volume turned to maximum and I could sense the sheer power of the water. Then, as we passed it by, the noise of the falling water faded away behind us and the river soon regained its more placid nature. The next landmark was the rickety old wooden bridge. Once we had crossed this, we were in prime mushroom country and if it was early in the morning we would deviate to pick mushrooms.

Mushrooms provided a good source of pocket money and even though I couldn't see where they were, just being part of the act made me a member of the team and carrying the bags entitled me to my share of the spoils. Not that anyone would have argued anyway. If they had caught fish and I hadn't, I still got my share; if we went out on Langness golf links looking for lost golf balls that we could sell on, I got my share; and so it was with the mushrooms as well. I took part in all these activities with the kids who lived on Janet's Corner, and even though they were often carrying a passenger in me, they treated me exactly as one of them. No wonder I missed home so much when I was at school. I didn't really hate St Vincent's or Liverpool, I simply loved home and the folks that made home so special. With the mushroom-picking complete, it would be onward towards Ballasalla. Apart from our own voices, the only sounds were the gently-flowing river as it danced its way over the stones on its journey to Castletown harbour, the wild birds, freely going about their business totally undisturbed by man or beast, and the sound of the occasional steam train as it puffed and clanked its way to Castletown. Upon reaching Ballasalla, my brother, Kevin, and I would branch off to go and visit my grandad and granny who lived in the village. Our mates would go and do their own thing and we would arrange to meet them later, to begin the homeward journey.

I always enjoyed visiting Granny and Grandad's place. He was forever chewing rubber and always had as much time as I needed, no matter what he was doing when my unannounced visit occurred. Granny always had interesting things to eat and for some strange reason, a biscuit or a cake in someone else's house always tasted better than it did in your own. I don't know why but every time I called at Granny's she seemed to be just about to get the Hoover out. Grandad hated the Hoover and as soon as he saw it coming, he would leg it out through the kitchen door, scooping me up with him. Once outside, we would sit on the grid in the garden, Grandad chewing on his rubber whist I updated him with my latest plans to escape from St Vincent's. I always left there with my spirits lifted, as he would tell me that he was going to go and see someone in the Government and talk to him or her about my plight. Well, I don't know if he ever did, but at least I felt better for knowing that my grandad was on my side.

Returning to school never got any easier. As I grew older, I understood it more and the reasons why it had to be this way, but right up to the age of sixteen I would start feeling miserable about three days before I was due to go back. I can never remember a going-back-to-school day on which I didn't shed a tear, although, as I grew older, the tears and the grief became more of a private matter.

If there was a coal boat in Castletown on such days, Dad's two brothers, Uncle Lenny and Uncle Willie, would be at our house early for a seven o'clock start, so the house would be full of activity from early morning. Mother would be busy making tea for Dad and his coal boat gang, whilst at the same time frantically running around, pushing last minute things into a suitcase for me. Before leaving to discharge the coal boat, both Uncle Lenny and Uncle Willie would rummage through their pockets and hand over their loose change to me. I remember on one of these occasions Dad had left home at about 6 a.m. to take the ropes off an incoming coal boat. Uncle Lenny and Uncle Willie both arrived at our house at about half past six for a mug of tea and to meet up with Dad, who was supposed to be coming back to the house for his breakfast before starting work on the boat. As my uncles sat in the house, they joked that they had seen Dad swimming like the clappers in the harbour, implying that he had fallen in. I refused point blank to leave home unless he returned so that I could see that he was okay. As the time for the bus taking us to the early morning boat drew nearer, Mother tried frantically to convince me that Dad was fine. I would have none of it; but with about two minutes to go, Dad turned up for his breakfast. I think in all my years of going back to school that was the only occasion on which I remember returning to school relatively happy. Uncle Willie was always happy, always singing, always telling jokes. Once both uncles had handed over to me their dinner money for that day, all five shillings of it, they would depart with that all too familiar sentence, one which I had heard over a thousand times: "You'll be home again in three months, it will soon pass."

If there was no coal boat in Castletown and Dad had managed to get someone else to work his shift at the Gas Works, he would take me back. This would be a slightly more laid-back affair. There would be no diving back to the house from the bus stop to collect something he had forgotten. No last minute panic with regard to lost boat tickets. I never wanted my two brothers to come out to the bus stop with me, I hated good-byes since they only brought on the tears, so, the fewer folks to say good-bye to, the better. I wanted to share with my brothers some of my untold wealth, which was often in excess of ten shillings, more money than they had ever had between the pair of them; but they always declined. Dad would never be still. On rough crossings he would juggle with cups of tea for both me, himself and any other passengers who weren't able to trust themselves to make it up the stairs to the buffet bar and back without spilling the lot. There would be a trip up on deck which lasted until I could not stand the wind any longer. Once it got to twelve o'clock, we would be nearing the Mersey Bar and the lack of vibration through the passenger lounge floor would tell me we were now much closer to Liverpool than to Douglas.

Arriving back at school was not the ordeal that it once was. I knew now where I was going, I knew which corridors to go down and I knew the staff. Also, I had mates there now as well and although the relationship with my schoolmates was not the same kind of relationship I had with my pals back in Castletown, nonetheless a bonding had taken place. However, there was still the homesickness problem that never went away and although I no longer had any fear of being far away in a strange place and I could look after myself, I still missed home desperately. It always took me several days to readjust to the way of school life. Although to all intent and purposes this was a special school for the blind, the truth was that there were very few actually blind kids in the school. Most of the pupils were partially sighted and it was these kids with whom I had bonded, rather than the totally blind kids. I guess the sighted kids were more similar to my mates at home. They were just that bit more active than the others. The majority of the blind kids seemed to be happy to spend most of their free time sitting on the school benches listening to the radio. I really don't know whether this listening to the radio had anything to do with being blind. In all schools there are kids who are more active than others, and maybe this was just a case in point. Generally the activities that took place at school were of a much more gentle nature than those I indulged in at home. There was certainly no rock climbing, no fishing, no beach to mess about on and almost all my free time would be confined to the school grounds. However, there was football.

Chapter Twelve

The football at St Vincent's was not played in the same competitive way as it was on the waste ground at Janet's Corner but that could hardly be expected. A blind teacher, Mr Frank McFarlain, nearly always attended our kick-around at St Vincent's. At the far end of the playground a large wooden board about the size of a goal-mouth had been erected. This meant that the ball could not be lost in a net, and when the ball had been banged past the goalkeeper, the sound of it hitting the wooden board would tell the goal scorer that he had scored. Ball bearings were placed inside the ball, just as was done at home. Once again, I always seemed to be the goalkeeper and I remember furious arguments taking place between me and Mr McFarlain as to whether it was a goal or not. On hearing his shot hit the wooden goal structure, or what he deemed to be the wooden goal structure, he would immediately award himself a goal. Sometimes his shot had hit me and sometimes I had even saved the ball. There is nothing worse when you have just made a blinding save than to have it denied you by the teacher, especially when your fingers or face are still stinging from the save. Our conversation would go something like this. McFarlain: "Goal!" Me: "No, sir." McFarlain: "Yes it was, Glassey." Me: "No it wasn't, sir, it hit me on the head." McFarlain: "Well I could tell by the sound of it that it had hit wood so the goal stands." Mind you, I guess on balance things evened out, as there was many an occasion when the ball did go past me and struck the wooden board and I argued that it hadn't and that I had made yet another of my blinding saves. As Mr McFarlain pointed out to me on more than one occasion, if I had made as many saves as I made out I would have played for Liverpool, blind or not.

Another football-related activity was the game of crab football. This was something that was pursued during school time, rather than in the playground. The game had more or less the same rules as football, only you played the game in a gym. You moved about the pitch in crab form, hands behind your back on the floor. The ball was two wicker baskets about the size of waste-paper baskets. Inside the baskets were placed some small tin lids for sound effects. The two baskets were then bound together in canvas and this was our crab football. We mostly played this strange form of football amongst ourselves during P.E. lessons, but sooner or later someone got the idea that it would be good for us to play other, sighted, schools. We already played the Blind School in Manchester once a year. The first match was to be against a grammar school and would be played over two legs, the first in their gym. Of course they had never played this game before, but even so, they really did not expect any serious opposition from the Blind School down the road. We had to bring our own ball, as of course they did not have anything remotely like a crab football. I think they went into a fair state of shock when they got their first glimpse of this ruddy great thing they were expected to kick around their gym in their pumps. There were six players in a crab football team and I was absolutely thrilled to be in our school team. The fact that they were a sighted school held no fears at all for me, as they were only the same kind of kids I knocked about with at home.

Although we were referred to as the Blind School, in fact the only blind kid in our team was me. Our striker was one of my best mates, not only at school but anywhere. His name was Charlie and he came from the north east of England. Later he made the odd trip home with me at half-term to the Isle of Man. Charlie had a fair amount of sight and was as athletic as any other kid from any other school. The poor grammar school got the shock of their lives as, straight from the kick off, me and my mate went in wild pursuit of those tin lids and fought for possession of them like lions. I am sure that their goalkeeper dived out of the way of the first shot at his goal as these bloody great baskets came hurtling towards him. We soon went 2-0 up with both goals coming from Charlie. I think the grammar school was nervous about hitting such a beast of a ball. They certainly would never have seen anything like it before or since, I shouldn't think, and I am sure they would have suffered severe embarrassment the next day in front of their chums for being defeated by the Blind School. I did speak with their goalkeeper afterwards and he expressed his surprise that they had only lost 2-0 as he had spent the whole match trying to get out of the way of the ball. We continued playing other schools at this crazy game, but the schools of Liverpool never really got hooked on it, hence we only ever lost one match.

It wasn't just my dedication to the school crab football team that was being observed at this time. The nuns had duly noted my seemingly renewed devotion towards the Church with regard to Mass attendance. I was always an early riser, even as a small child I never had any difficulty with getting up in the mornings. Sister Cissy would call us at 7-30, allowing half an hour to dress and wash before an 8 a.m. breakfast. I would often lie awake for over an hour before this time, but the only way I would be permitted to rise earlier than anyone else would be if I was to attend the 7 a.m. Mass. Mass was said every day of the week at 7 a.m. Monday to Saturday and at 8 a.m. on Sundays. The only Mass that was compulsory for us kids to attend was the 8 a.m. Mass on Sundays. And so it was that I decided to rise early at about 6 a.m. and attend Mass. The Mass itself was boring, but not as boring as lying in bed and so I rose with the lark every day and took my pew in the back of the little school chapel. This devotion of mine was wrongly but understandably interpreted by the nuns as a clear indication of my faith, and possibly that the message was starting finally to get through to me. Sisters I didn't even know very well were now stopping me in the school corridors as I went about my daily business and engaging me in conversation.

My pal, Andy, who had accompanied me on these early morning jaunts was experiencing the same treatment. Neither Andy nor myself were regarded as being devout churchgoers by the rest of our school pals. What the nuns and our school pals didn't realise was that Andy and I both regarded going to early morning Mass as a price worth paying. It presented us with opportunities that would not have come our way had we stayed in bed until the normal getting up time. At 6 a.m., while all the other kids lay in their beds, the long corridors of the convent would be deserted. The playrooms and rest-rooms would be unsupervised, leaving the way clear for Andy and me to rummage

72

through cupboards. We'd find cakes and biscuits and so on, placed there by staff for some future use. There were also plenty of little hide-aways in the playgrounds and a playing field in which to go and have a crafty smoke in practically total safety. We had about half an hour before and after Mass to indulge in these activities. The going to Mass was essential, as no one was allowed to rise before Sister Cissy appeared in the dormitory at 7.30. We had to inform Sister Cissy the night before that we were attending Mass the following morning; this way she could keep a check to see if anyone had left their bed without authorisation. Andy and I were more than happy to attend Mass every morning in return for a feed of cake and biscuits and a crafty fag both before and after Mass. Of course, our devotion did not go unnoticed by the powers that be, and in due course the Mother Superior, Sister Claire, sent for us both.

It was not unusual for me or for Andy to be sent for by the Mother Superior or by the head teacher, and as we both made our way along the corridor to Sister Claire's office we pondered as to what we might have done. Maybe we had been seen smoking or maybe the missing cakes had been traced to the two every-day-Mass-going boys. We both stood in Sister Claire's office waiting for the lecture and the punishment to be meted out. "It has been noted," she began, "that the pair of you have not missed a Mass for several months and in recognition of this it has been decided that both of you are to become altar boys." She went on to explain to us about what an honour it was to be made altar boys, indeed it was one of the most sought-after privileges in the school. As we both stepped out into the corridor from Sister Claire's office, we could not believe what had just happened to us. Neither I nor Andy had bargained for being made altar boys. Neither of us was hooked on religion and we both stood at the back of the school chapel every morning bored sick and not taking part in the service. I did feel a few pangs of guilt, for as a result of our cake and biscuit nicking, and a few crafty fags, we had now been rewarded with this prestigious honour. Also, our early morning treat of cake and biscuits would now be turned into something of a feast, as from now on we would have access to wine as well. Smoking, feasting and boozing, at 6 a.m. in the morning and in a convent school, who would have believed it! This kind of thing wouldn't even happen at home and I don't think any of my mates at home would have believed me if I had told them that, before school most mornings, we spent our time feasting on cakes, smoking fags and knocking back a glass of wine or two!

As altar boys, we had to be in the chapel before anyone else in order to get everything ready for the priest to say Mass. Andy and I would help ourselves to a glass of wine. I think we thought it helped us to get into the spirit of things. Most of the time we would only have one glass but occasionally we might have two and on one occasion we had a real binge. Indeed I think it was that binge that finally led to our relatively short careers at the altar. I don't think either Andy or I looked on it as an honour to serve at the altar; it simply meant that the Mass was not so boring as when we were sitting in one of the pews. We certainly did not see it as taking our first steps towards priesthood. I think our dismissal had been on the cards for quite a while, even before Andy puked up one day on the altar during the Mass because of a slightly heavier drinking bout before Mass in the sacristy. I do not remember any great fuss being made of us being fired. We simply were not selected any more. There was no big announcement or anything like that. As far as I know we were the only boys who used to be altar boys. In most cases when lads became altar boys they remained so until the end of their school days. I never did like wine and still don't to this day; it was simply a case of don't eat the forbidden fruit. At the time of our binges the wine had not been consecrated, which must have meant at worst that we were only guilty of under-age drinking and not the more serious sin of abusing the Lord's blood. However, I do recall relating to someone at one time how Andy and I were in fact holier than the priest himself, as we had a great deal more of the Lord's blood in us than he had. During the service he would only take a small sip as opposed to our several glasses downed in the sacristy before the start of Mass!

Chapter Thirteen

The half-term breaks were now beginning to take a different twist. My mother's three brothers, Louis, Sean and Tommy, had all left Ireland and set themselves up in London. Uncle Louis, who had left Tipperary with little more than his fare to London, had now worked his way up and owned a building firm that employed over six hundred men. My Uncle Tommy was working as a site manager for him, and Uncle Sean, who had gone to London as a coach driver, had bought his own coach. At half-term, Mother and sometimes Father would come over from the Island and we would all make our way down to London. Uncle Tommy didn't drive, so it was always Louis or Sean who would drive up to the school, having first picked up Mother or Father, or both, from the boat. When Uncle Louis came it was always in style, the Jag or the Merc. Of course we were not accustomed to being driven about in such luxurious modes of transport. I am not sure what the nuns made of it all. From their point of view, last term I had to stay at school because we couldn't afford the boat fare home. This term I was setting off to London in a Jag or a Merc and seemingly money was no object.

Speeding down the motorway to London from Liverpool was not quite the same as crossing the Irish Sea by boat, and it certainly wasn't the same as going home. But it wasn't a bad second best. We usually stayed in Louis's house with his wife, Joan, and their five kids. It was a huge house with more than one bathroom; I had never known a house to have more than one bathroom. There was also a phone; I had never stayed in a house with its own phone before. The phone never stopped ringing; men querying their wages, site managers looking for Louis and contractors from building sites all over London looking for Louis. He was indeed one of the biggest building contractors in London and the phone would keep ringing until well after midnight with his unwearying wife, Joan, never tiring of answering it. Several years earlier Louis had simply got on his bike and rode away from his parents' home in Ireland and made his way to London. He arrived with nothing, but once there everything he touched seemed to turn to gold. In due course his two brothers Sean and Tommy followed him to London and both thrived on his success. Tommy worked as a joiner and as a foreman on Louis's sites for the whole of Louis's reign in London, whilst Sean eventually took up driving coaches for a well-known coach proprietor before he eventually went on to buy his own coach.

The life style in London was a completely new ball game to me. It was a million miles away from the much more mundane and less sophisticated sleepy Castletown. Louis drove around in flash cars, wore expensive clothes, wined and dined in London's top restaurants. Joan wore expensive jewellery and their five kids had every toy in creation. I was given fivers for pocket money. Louis would always make sure his two brothers, Sean and Tommy, were present as he pulled out a fiver and thrust it into my hand, knowing full well that the other two would have to follow suit. Now I was a millionaire too. As a lad of about twelve or thirteen with £15 in my pocket in the 1960s I had joined the jet set. Yes, London meant untold wealth and for a kid it held many fascinations, but it wasn't Castletown; it was big, busy and dirty, and it wasn't home.

For some reason, it always seemed to be Uncle Sean who drove us back from the half-term stint in London. It was always an early start around 6 a.m. as going back to school had to coincide with Mother and Father first being taken to the Pier Head for the 11 a.m. sailing to Douglas. This meant that I would be back in school at about 12 p.m., long before any of the other kids. I didn't really mind this; it was not as if I had come from home and I didn't have that horrible sickly feeling in the pit of my stomach that I used to get when returning to school from home. Uncle Sean had a heart of gold, and his generosity towards me as a child knew no bounds and he has continued in that vein right up until the present day. Before dropping me back at the school he would slip me another fiver, over and above the one he had given me in London when being shamed by Louis. In truth, I don't believe Louis had ever shamed him into giving me anything. He had a very generous nature and would have given of his own free will, anyway.

I remember once returning to school after one of these London jaunts with £12 in my pocket. This was as much as Dad earned in the Gas Works as a week's wages, and I was probably the richest kid in the school for a short period. I decided not to hand over my loot to the nuns, as I didn't see much point in having so much money and then being restricted to two or three shillings a week. In any case I could manage my fortune much better than they could. Hanging on to this fortune was something of a pointless exercise really as I couldn't spend it in the school tuck shop, or at the weekend when we were being taken out by the teachers since my somewhat lavish life style would have been noticed. So, I kept it because it made me feel better knowing that at least I knew that if the chance ever came my way, I had enough money for my escape boat fare or whatever. Over a period of time, the money was gradually frittered away and was usually well spent before the end of term.

In London, Uncle Louis continued to amass his fortune, although I only came into contact with him when he made the occasional visit to the Isle of Man, or on those sporadic half-term trips to London. As for Uncle Sean, well, that was a different matter. He had instructed me to phone his home in London once a week, reversing the charges, which I did every Saturday. Whenever his coach journeys brought him north, he would make his way out to the school to visit me, sometimes having to drive 20 or 30 miles out of his way to do so. This also caused me to be the centre of attention, as not only did I turn up at the school with the occasional sea captain and roar off to London in posh cars but, now and then, empty coaches would turn up to visit me. I think my status in the school had now changed from someone who came with nothing, to someone who had somehow made good and was now something of an executive pupil!

Chapter Fourteen

My executive status was further enhanced by a change that was to be made in my travel arrangements. From now on, I was to fly to and from school at the end of each term. The Isle of Man Government would pay for this air travel and I guess it was cheaper than paying someone to travel over by boat, stay in a hotel and travel back with me the next day. From now on, I would be taken to the airport by a member of staff from school, put on a plane and met at the other end by someone from home. The same thing would happen in reverse going back. This would be great for going home as I would now be home in half an hour and, more importantly, I would be home the same day and not lose a day by having to stay overnight in a Liverpool hotel. However, it was not good from a going back point of view. I would be back at school within an hour of leaving home. Up until now the boat had provided me with a four-hour transitional period in which to adjust. My love affair with the Isle of Man Steam Packet was not at an end. I would still use the boat at half-terms as Mother and Father still had to meet the expenses of half-term travel.

On my first flight home I was, however, accompanied by Mother. I don't know why, it must have been deemed by the powers that be that I would be better off accompanied for the first trip. Despite many flights to and from the Island, I have never developed a passion for air travel or a fascination with aircraft as I did for the sea. Nonetheless, I do clearly remember my first journey home by air. It was going-home-day once again and I remember sitting on the bench

One of Cambrian Airways' Viscounts which provided the author with an alternative to the usual sea travel at the beginning and end of school terms.

in the main corridor outside the school clinic. I was even more excited than normal this time as I was not going to be spending a night in a Liverpool hotel and losing a precious day of my holiday. The kids were all running up and down the corridor in that usual going-home-day excitement. I remember Mrs Pope, one of my teachers, walking up to me and saying, "I suppose you will not be leaving until tomorrow, Thomas," "No, Miss," I replied, "I am flying home tonight at five o'clock." I was not just excited about going home. This time it was because I was travelling by plane as well. I imagined an aeroplane to be something like a bus but I simply could not sort out in my head just what this bus would be like. None of my brothers had ever flown and none of my mates had either. In fact I didn't know anyone who had ever been on an aeroplane and I was going to be something of a celebrity when I got home.

Mother duly arrived and we set off to Liverpool city centre to do some shopping. Mother didn't have much in the way of money to spend, but I think she enjoyed just looking around the big stores in

Liverpool. In the 1960s the air services to the Isle of Man from Liverpool were operated by Cambrian Airways. They flew from Liverpool to Belfast, stopping off at the Isle of Man en route. As a child I had visited our local airport at Ronaldsway many times and loved sitting in the departure lounge listening to the announcements, but glad that I was not travelling myself. Nonetheless, I was still excited with the thought of my first 'plane trip and my fear of flying was overcome that day by the fact that I was flying home, I would be home the same day. Tonight I would be playing on the beach with Kevin and my mates and not stuck in some Liverpool hotel.

As I sat in my seat of the Cambrian Airways Viscount aircraft, I thought of how comfy the seats were. The floor of the aircraft was carpeted and I remember thinking to myself, as I explored the upholstery on the back of the seat in front of me with my fingers, that this plane is too nice to crash. It would be such a shame if all these posh seats were soaked by sea water. Yes, everything was going to be just fine. I also recall the announcement made by the stewardess, telling us where the life jackets were and how to use them. She went on and on about pulling them over your head and threading the cord around your chest and pulling some sort of toggle. At this point I remember thinking, "Crumbs, Mother will never manage this, why the hell didn't she send Dad!" Soon after we took off from Liverpool the stewardess brought drinks around and I was offered orange juice. I declined this on the grounds that I would not have time to drink it. By some queer logic known only to an air-frightened child, in refusing the juice I was telling myself that there was not enough time to drink it and therefore the flight would be over all the quicker.

The Viscount glided down through the Manx evening sky; soon, we touched down at Ronaldsway Airport and once again I was home. However, this homecoming by air was not the same as an arrival by sea. Stepping on to the tarmac at Ronaldsway was not quite the same as stepping off the gangway and on to the pier at Douglas. There was many an occasion when I could have kissed the ground when stepping on to the King Edward or Victoria Pier at Douglas, but I never got such a desire with the tarmac at Ronaldsway. Nevertheless, I was home after a short thirty-minute flight and I had not lost a day's holiday by having to stay overnight in Liverpool. Of course, I had heard the noise of aircraft passing over our house, which was only half a mile from the airport, and I had often wondered what it must be like to be in one. Well, now I knew. I could now tell my brothers and my mates what planes were like, and then get back to boats.

Chapter Fifteen

The summer holiday of 1967 was a bit special. I was thirteen years old and in September I would be fourteen. This meant that when I went back to school I would be eligible for my "permission". At St Vincent's, "permission", which was granted to kids as soon as they reached the age of fourteen, meant that you could go out on your own, unaccompanied by a member of school staff. It only applied at week-ends, but it did mean that as soon as I returned I would be able to roam Liverpool freely. I could go wherever I pleased and although it would still be a wrench to leave Castletown in September, at least this time I would have something to look forward to. But for now there was a whole seven-week summer holiday to enjoy and every single day of it was going to be like Christmas Day.

Just as change was on its way at St Vincent's in Liverpool, so too were things changing in Castletown. I was no longer confined to the Castletown area for my leisure activities. From now on I would be allowed to venture to such places as Douglas and Port Erin on the bus with my younger brother, Kevin. The whole gang, which included Billy Ronan, the son of the captain I referred to earlier, and the two brothers, Michael and Brian Christian, who lived just across the road from us, would usually set off on these adventures. I could never tire of such places as Langness, with its acres of open space for me to roam over freely; or Castletown beach, which I often had entirely to myself to run on the sand or to scramble over the slippery rocks; or Castletown itself, with its quiet, narrow streets where a blind child could wander through the nooks and crannies in more or less perfect safety. Notwithstanding all these things, the trips to Douglas were exciting, special treats, and they are as fresh in my mind today as if they had just happened yesterday. With a few shillings in our pockets, brother Kev, Billy, Brian, Michael and myself would head off for Douglas. I always got a buzz from the bus ride alone on our trips to Douglas; there was that feel-good feeling knowing I was not going for the nine o'clock boat. Stepping off the bus in Douglas bus station, I would get a tingle in my bones, the special kind of excitement that you can only find in a busy holiday resort in the middle of summer.

I loved the noise that came from the busy shop doorways as we scurried past on our march through Strand Street. There was the smell of burgers, hot-dogs and chips wafting through the air, and the latest chart sounds of the Beatles and Cliff Richard coming from the record shops. Throngs of people were everywhere. Sometimes, I would hear the most wonderful sound - the shrill of the steam whistle from one of the Steam Packet vessels about to depart, even more wonderfully, without me on board. We would go on to the promenade for the three-mile walk along its entire length until we reached our destination, the White City fair ground.

We would take the seaward side of the prom. As we walked, I could hear the 'clip clop' of the horse trams on my left-hand side, whilst on my right there was the sound of the sea as it gently washed the Douglas shoreline. Thousands of delighted shrieks of enjoyment would drift up from the water's edge. Douglas was full of happy holiday makers and the feel of the hot summer sun on my face, along with the shrieks of joy coming up from the beach, together with the rattle of the horse trams trundling along the prom, made me feel good to be alive. Eventually we would reach the White City fair ground. As soon as we entered this magical place of fun, I would be totally transfixed by the atmosphere of the place. There was the siren of the ghost train screaming out above everything else, the sound of the dodgem cars as they smashed into one another, and the distant pop, pop, pop of the motor boats as they cruised their way around the boating lake. The air was full of the sound of happy people and you didn't need to be wealthy to feel that you were the happiest kid on the planet.

Kevin, Billy, Michael and Brian would have a go on every stall, be it throwing hoops at targets or knocking bottles over with small balls. At the end of it they would count up all their prizes and share them with me. Even though I had not won any of them, I would usually end up with more prizes than they had. The same rules applied on the fair ground as applied on the mushroom fields or when we were collecting golf balls. They shared everything they had with me, the gang was totally as one. No wonder I didn't want to go away to school; I didn't have any brothers over there, and I would not find mates like these lads anywhere else in the world.

Although I was now going to places such as Douglas, all the other activities did not get neglected. There was still the odd shift at the Gas Works to put in, and my visits to the coal boats took precedence over anything else. My neighbour and close friend, Michael Quine, had now taken up work with the Steam Packet, and this would prove to be very beneficial to me when I returned to school in September. In the meantime, I would often take a trip with him in his small 13-foot wooden boat, which he kept berthed in Castletown harbour. There was not an awful lot of activity on a Sunday on the Isle of Man in those days. I recall one Sunday afternoon when Dad decided to join us for a quick trip around the bay. Dad was not a sailor and so it was a rare thing for him to join us on such jaunts. However, I remember him on this occasion commenting to Michael about the racket the boat's outboard engine was making as we motored out of Castletown harbour. He was concerned that someone might complain about the noise we were making on a Sunday. How attitudes change! Now a bomb could go off in the middle of the town square and hardly anyone would blink.

Other things were now starting to interest me, including photography. This might seem strange, but for some reason I developed a fascination with the camera. I remember the week-end when my two rich uncles, Louis and Sean, came from London to stay with us. Needless to say, I ended up with more pocket money than I was accustomed to. With money in my pocket, I took myself off to Peggy Watterson's toyshop and bought myself a smart little camera for four shillings and sixpence. I don't recall Peggy asking me why I wanted the camera, or the local chemist asking me why I wanted a film. Anyway, off I went taking photographs all over town. I took snaps of coal boats, the river, the steam trains and friends. Later, when I got my film back from the chemist having had it developed, I was not at all dismayed that none of my photos had come out! After all, what did my friends know anyway. The photos may not have come out as far as they were concerned, but I could find absolutely nothing wrong with them! They were about six inches long and four inches wide. They were smooth on one side and glossy on the other and, of course, they were photographs. They felt just like any other photo, and as far as I was concerned they were just as good as anyone else's.

Rich uncles from London were not the only way of raising much needed funds in those days and our gang was not short of enterprise. Bottles provided a very handy source of income. The problem was finding enough of them. For every bottle we handed over the shop counter, we would receive threepence so, with this in mind, bottle thieving was big business. A considerable bounty was to be had through the local pub, The Duck's Nest. This pub kept all its empty bottles in crates around the back of the building; and I, accompanied by my brother Kevin, and Brian and Michael, would sneak around the back and carefully select the pop bottles. We only took pop bottles, as we knew we would get no joy from the landlord if we knocked on the pub door and tried to pass him beer bottles. Of course, it didn't take the landlord long to work out that bottles he had previously paid out on and placed in crates behind the pub were coming back to him for a second pay out, and we were sent packing. The trick then was to take bottles from one pub or shop and offer them to another. It came as no surprise to me when the cash-back for bottles scheme ground to a halt. In that September of 1967 my brother Lenny only had one term left before leaving school. He got a job straight away working for Downwards, the lemonade factory in Douglas. What a shame they had done away with the cash-back for bottles system by then. We would have been tax exiles with the money we would have made as he brought home almost as much pop as the factory produced. The tin can has much to answer for; not only did it do away with our small bottles, but it is also non-returnable.

Of course, there were still the lost golf balls to be rounded up from Langness golf course and sold on. Then Billy, who I guess was the gang's chief executive, had also worked out how, by the use of a knife, pennies could be retrieved from the door of the public toilet. This means of funding never really amounted to very much; the coin-collecting mechanism in the door often proved somewhat reluctant to give up its contents, and this, together with the noise the knife made extracting what was never more than a small amount of cash, meant that it was eventually given up as a high-risk, low-paying enterprise.

We realised that we needed a more regular income, and both Billy and Kevin did paper rounds for the two newsagents in Castletown. For this they received about twelve shillings and sixpence a week, and, of course, I accompanied one or the other of them, and sometimes both, carrying the paper bag on my shoulder for the duration of the round. They shared their wages with me, and I guess I was doing my bit, but in truth they would both have been able to complete their task much quicker on their bikes. Still, at least, in September, when it was time for me to return to school, their wages would shoot up and they would get the work done a little faster. Well, money isn't everything and it certainly wasn't then, for they both shed just as many tears as I did when the time came for me to return to Liverpool.

The school summer holiday passed all too quickly. Having spent the last couple of months fishing off piers, swimming in the sea, rambling on Langness, and sailing with Michael in his small boat, not to mention putting in the odd shift at the Gas Works and the hours and hours just sitting on the quayside at Castletown absorbing the goings on of the harbour, it was little wonder that going back to school was a depressing thought. The difference this time to my returning to St Vincent's would be that I would be going by air and unaccompanied. I would simply be taken to the airport, put on the plane, and met in Liverpool by one of the teachers.

Chapter Sixteen

My return to school this time was a whole new ball game. Returning by air didn't have the same drama as returning by sea. There was no early start to the day as my flight was not until eleven o'clock in the morning. My brothers had left for school before I did, but my parents accompanied me to the airport, which was within walking distance of our house. Our good-byes were said and, with a hug and a kiss, it was all over. Just over thirty minutes later I was in Liverpool and soon I was battering on Sister Claire's office door with my letter granting my mother and father's permission for me to be allowed out from school on my own. "So, Thomas, you have been back with us five or ten minutes at the most, and your first request is to be allowed out again." "Yes, Sister," I replied. "Well, you are fourteen years of age now, so from now on you can leave the grounds of this school whenever you like, so long as it is not in school time." "But Sister!" I exclaimed, "I thought this was only for week-ends." "No, Thomas, you are now free to leave as you wish, like I said, provided it is out of school hours." I was beside myself with excitement. I was free to go right now. Where the hell was Andy? I lost no time in finding him and giving him the news, and five minutes later Andy had returned from Sister Claire's office having been given the same pep talk. Ten minutes after that Andy, and I were walking down the school drive together, out through the gates. For the first time since I joined the school some nine years previously, I was a free man in Liverpool. I think my first day of being allowed out on my own was the happiest

The author, now aged 14, with his mother, Nel.

miserable day of my life. First days back at school were by their very nature miserable days: but to be happy on a miserable day was a really strange feeling. It was a bit like being happy even though you weren't meant to be. I had to remind myself that this was my first day back and, well, maybe school was going to be not quite so bad after all. Of course I had known that this privilege was coming, but I had thought it only applied at week-ends and this was an unexpected bonus.

I was now fourteen and a senior pupil, which meant that not only were the week-ends going to be more fulfilling, but also that school in general was improving. I would be allowed to stay up until half past nine; and at four o'clock, when the school day finished, we would be given bread and jam and mugs of tea. This might sound mundane enough, but it was a real treat after having endured nine years of a strict regime of breakfast, dinner and supper all eaten at exactly their appointed times and in the formal surroundings of the dining-room. The tea and jam butties served up in the playroom gave the place a homely sort of atmosphere. Also from now on I would be allowed to wear my own clothes out of school hours. My pocket money would be increased to four shillings a week, which meant that I could spend one and eightpence on ten fags and have two and fourpence to spend on whatever I liked. Of course, the pocket money increase was only available provided you had the funds sent from home to meet it. My school pals were a great bunch of lads and if any of us, for any reason, found ourselves without funds on pay day, which was Friday, we would always muck in and I don't remember anyone ever going without. We did have other ways of supplementing our income and one of these was by the holy souls box.

The holy souls, we were told, were folks who had died with sin on their souls and were therefore not allowed to enter the Kingdom of Heaven until God had forgiven them their sins. I am as much baffled today as I was then as to why the nuns had placed a collection box in the porch of the school chapel for the holy souls. We pupils could not for the life of us see how the nuns could get this (probably much needed) cash to Purgatory, which apparently was where the holy souls were languishing. One of the hymns sung on a regular basis at St Vincent's was called, "Those holy souls, they suffer on", and it was this hymn that Andy and I sang as we helped ourselves to a handful of coppers from the holy souls collection box, which we passed when setting off for one of our Saturday jaunts. We were never caught in this theft, but then the fact that it was a collection box meant that the nuns would never have known exactly how much was in it anyway. What also puzzled us kids was just exactly who was putting the money in there; it was certainly not going short and I can only presume that it must have been the nuns themselves. At any rate, we never did find out who emptied it or how they paid it in. Maybe there are some things you are simply better off not knowing. Anyway, it's a good thing that folks don't go straight to Heaven, for it was many a time that those holy souls came to our rescue with a packet of fags, a bottle of pop or a bar of chocolate. I am still to this day very grateful to them.

We got away with robbing the holy souls, but, alas, we were not so lucky with St Dominic. I don't know why we had a snooker table in the playroom of a blind school, but a snooker table we had. I don't remember anyone ever trying to play snooker on it, but I do remember that on the bank of lockers next to the snooker table was a lifesize

statue of St Dominic. It was during one lunch time that St Dominic came down from the top of the lockers, dressed himself up in a blazer, school tie and a pair of sun glasses, with a snooker cue resting in his hand, which was also clutching a Bible, and a Woodbine hanging from his mouth. Standing next to the snooker table, he really looked the part. As Andy and I answered the school bell for the afternoon session, making our way slowly along the school corridor, we heard Sister Cissy's shrieks of dismay as her eyes fell on the figure standing at the snooker table. I don't know which shocked her most, the fact that someone was for the first time in her experience actually having a quiet game of snooker, or that it was St Dominic who had come down from the lockers, dressed himself in suitable attire and lit himself a Woodbine.

I knew that the nuns believed in miracles; they frequently had told me so in umpteen religious lessons, but not, it seems, when faced with one in their own backyard or, should I say, playroom. The history lesson had not long started when the classroom door opened and the school secretary asked if Tom Glassey could make his way to the Mother Superior's office. I don't know why I had been found guilty without a trial, but guilty I surely was, trial or not. I don't know which offence was the more serious; the fact that I had taken a statue, which had no doubt been blessed by the priest, and dressed it in a totally inappropriate manner, or the fact that it had a Woodbine in its mouth. That, of course, meant that I had the forbidden weed in a place where it was an offence just to have a distant relative who smoked, let alone smoke yourself; and if St Dominic had been caught smoking in the playroom, and if I had given him the cigarette, then I must be smoking as well. As Sister Claire considered my punishment, my heart sank. My recently-gained "permission" now hung by a thread. I didn't have to wait long for the verdict. "Thomas, you will receive no pocket money for three weeks. If you can't afford to buy cigarettes, then in three weeks you should be well on your way to curing your addiction." I left her office breathing a great sigh of relief. I would get

(Facing page) When home, the author never missed the opportunity of supporting his football heroes of Castletown F.C. Here is the team of 1967-68. Back row, left to right: Alan Phillips, Bill Beech, Willie McHarrie, Ron Ronan, Denis Moore and Tony Birch. Front row: Trevor Taubman, Dave Wilkinson, Joe Ennett, Eddie Ardern, Paul Baker and Sid Butler.

sixpence off each of my mates; and as for the short fall, well, let's say thank goodness the nuns believed not everyone went straight to Heaven when they died. Those holy souls would suffer on a little longer.

Week-ends at St Vincent's were now something to be looked forward to, and Saturdays just couldn't come round quickly enough. Once dinner had been eaten, we were off for the afternoon. Most Saturdays were spent around the dock area of the city; but occasionally we would go to Anfield to see Liverpool playing at home. We could not do this too often as it was four shillings to stand on the Kop and that was the cheapest part of the ground. Going to Anfield wasn't a new experience for me as I had been several times when I was younger, and had even been to the house of one of Liverpool's footballers, Chris Lawler. Quite a few of the Liverpool players had been out to the school, and had attended events such as Christmas parties; and I had been taken to many reserve matches by both players and friends. However, to go of our own accord and stand on the Kop with the die-hards was somewhat more rewarding than being up in the main stand under someone else's guidance. Not being able to see the game made absolutely no difference to me at all. Being packed in with fifty thousand fans all singing and shouting was an enriching experience on its own, and wouldn't my mates back home in Castletown give anything to swap places with me. In truth, they would have had no problem in swapping places with me, for as much as I loved going to Anfield, home had a much greater pull on my heart strings and I would have at any time gladly given up my place on the Kop for a place in the tiny grandstand in Castletown's football ground at Malew Road.

Every pupil of St Vincent's was given a free bus-pass which not only enabled us to use the buses throughout the city but also the Mersey ferries. This pass was worth its weight in gold as it meant that even when funds were stretched we could still put in a full day gallivanting around Liverpool. As soon as Saturday's one o'clock dinner was over, I, together with Andy and Noel, a lad from County Armagh, would set off for the Pier Head. Once there, it was straight to the landing stage to check out which of the Isle of Man steamers was lying alongside. In summertime, whichever steamer had taken the morning sailing from Douglas would be lying there making ready to head back to Douglas at 3.30 p.m; and there would often be more than one vessel alongside. The landing stage would be awash with passengers either disembarking or boarding for the afternoon sailing. If I was present on the stage as the afternoon steamer pulled away, I would always get a lump in the throat as she pulled out into the river and sounded that all too familiar triple-bell steam-whistle. It was almost as if she wanted to rub salt into my wounds. In a bid to regain control over my emotions, I would turn to Andy and Noel and suggest a trip across the river on one of the ferries.

On winter Saturdays, in contrast to summertime, the Pier Head was much quieter. The Steam Packet vessel that had sailed from Douglas that morning would be lying there right through until Monday, and the only people milling around would be those using the Mersey ferries. As far as I was concerned, however, winter was certainly the best time of the year for our trips to the Pier Head. There may have been only one vessel alongside there but the rest of the fleet would be laid up over the river in the Morpeth Dock in Birkenhead. Sometimes we would take the ferry across the Mersey and go and explore the docks on the Birkenhead side. I would lead my gang of troops aboard but of course these ship were now largely deserted and just lay silent in the dock. They were ghostly quiet and almost creepy, like trees that had lost their leaves in winter. They lay barren and bare, stripped of all their fittings for the winter overhaul and a far cry from the summer when all their sleeping and silent limbs would burst into life and they would be in full bloom, their decks thronged with passengers.

Week-ends at the Pier Head meant that I had two days to visit a little piece of home, even if it was floating in the Mersey and tied up to the Prince's Landing Stage. In order to gain access to it, it was necessary to get past the duty policeman in his box. I would explain to him that we were visiting friends who were crew members aboard the ship. I would then reel off the captain's name, along with the names of just about everyone I knew from Castletown who was working with the Steam Packet, or had done so at some point in the past. I think the policeman was halfway up the gangway of the ship to check my story as I was still reeling off my list of 'who's who' with the Isle of Man Steam Packet Company. He would return to his box and motion us towards the gangway. Once on board, I would enquire to see if Captain Jack was aboard, or Michael, my neighbour from

Castletown. Captain Jack would always respond very positively and give the boys and me a full tour of the ship. Of course, this was nothing new to me, but to the boys from St Vincent's, who in most cases had never been on board a ship before apart from the Mersey ferries, it was brilliant. Once word got around the school about my unofficial guided tours of these ships, interest grew and on occasions I would turn up with as many as six or seven lads from the school for Captain Jack to entertain. To his eternal credit he never shirked these extra, unpaid duties bestowed on him by the blind kids of St Vincent's.

I recall one summer Saturday afternoon when I went on board the Steam Packet vessel, *King Orry*. On this occasion, Michael Quine was on board and on seeing me he invited me to sail with the vessel the next day on a day trip to Llandudno, and, of course, I took him up on this offer. However, the following morning I turned up at the landing stage with no fewer than six of my schoolmates! Naturally, we were all welcomed on board and enjoyed a full day's hospitality with the crew of the *King Orry*. Looking back on this trip, and on the unofficial tours of inspection of Steam Packet vessels carried out by my classmates and myself, we must at times have been a right pain in the neck to the busy crews of these ships. But never once did they ask us to leave the ship; and they always seemed to make enough time to deal with our demands.

In the summer months, the Steam Packet boats were only alongside for a couple of hours and there would not be enough time for us to go aboard, so we would spend all Saturday afternoon sailing to and fro across the Mersey on the ferry. It wasn't everyone's cup of tea, but what a wonderful way to put in a day for a ship-mad schoolboy. Sometimes, one of the mighty C.P.R. liners would be alongside the landing stage. With the little Mersey ferries coming and going every ten minutes or so, the Steam Packet vessels departing for Douglas, and one of the C.P.R. liners getting ready to sail for Montreal, the Prince's Landing Stage would be a hive of activity. I would often be happy just to stand there in a state of total wonderment at all that was going on around me.

It wasn't just Prince's Landing Stage that had a fascination for me; there was the dock network itself. We would often stroll through the docks and simply walk up the gangway of a vessel and plonk ourselves down on the deck. I remember a day when three or four of us walked aboard a cargo ship that was neither discharged nor loaded. After some time had elapsed and we had made ourselves at home, a group of men gathered about us all gabbling away in German. Of course, we did not understand what they were saying but they did seem to be getting just a touch excitable. After a while, we all got up and simply walked off the ship. As we walked down the gangway we could hear our German friends getting more and more excited. When we thought about it later we came to the conclusion that the German crew had probably been pointing and gesticulating towards the gangway, trying to shoo us off the ship, without having a clue that we were all blind. Of course, we had been totally unaware of this and we'd carried on sitting around the deck as if nothing was happening. It would only have been when we got up to leave the ship that it would have become apparent to the German crew that they had four blind visitors!

By the time I had reached the age of fourteen, I suppose my course was pretty well set. I was certainly not going to be a great academic, but I had done reasonably well. I had usually finished second and occasionally first in the end of term tests and I had good relations with the other kids and teachers. I was always sailing close to the wind with regards to school discipline, however. I had been caught smoking on many occasions, and at times I had been found outside the school grounds, well outside the school limits. I wasn't a really bad egg, but I certainly wasn't the kind of kid they made into a school prefect. I was never shipwrecked, but I had sailed in some rough waters and dangerously close to the rocks at times. However, my long voyage through school was now nearing its end. Still a few miles to go, but the shore was now in sight and the waters had certainly calmed.

I continued to fly home for the end-of-term holidays when the Government was paying, and to sail home for the half-term breaks when Dad was paying. I now travelled alone by both air and sea. I would be taken to the airport and put on a plane and picked up at the other end. On the boat it was the same principle, the only difference being, of course, that it was a much longer trip and being looked after by a ship's steward meant endless supplies of tea, sweets and sandwiches.

Chapter Seventeen

L ife was changing in Castletown. Activity at the Gas Works was coming to an end as it was no longer economical to ship coal in to the Island and then extract gas from it by means of a gas works in every town. Instead, gas was to be brought in by tanker and then piped from one central point to the whole Island. The "Ben" boats, so many of which Dad had emptied, had also changed. Gone were the small steamers that had plied these often hostile waters and frequented Castletown harbour since 1913. They were replaced by larger motor vessels, which were much better for their crews in terms of comfort, but lacked the character of the small steamers. In spite of this, I would never miss the opportunity to go aboard whenever one was discharging. My older brother, Lenny, was now well ensconced in the employ of the Downward's pop factory in Douglas. Kevin was earning his own pocket money by means of his paper round and by caddying out on Castletown golf links, so with a little more cash coming into the house things were improving.

The school holidays carried on in much the same vein; and we still spent long hours on the beach as it continued to hold a fascination for me. One new addition was the occasional day trip. It seemed inconceivable while I was at school that I would waste one day of my holiday at home by coming back to Liverpool. But on my first return day trip, to Liverpool with my younger brother, Kevin, I did just that. It was a revelation. For one thing, I got a bit of a kick out of going to Liverpool of my own accord; for another, I knew that I would soon be coming back, and it was a wonderful feeling sailing out on the 9 a.m. steamer knowing that I would be returning on the midnight sailing. I remember another of these day trips, but this time to Dublin. On this occasion, Mother made the trip with us so that she could visit her sister, Kathleen, who lived in Dublin. Whilst roaming around the decks of the *Manxman,* Kevin and I thought it might be nice to go and have our dinner in the ship's dining saloon. In those days the Steam Packet ships offered a silver-service dining arrangement. There was no plastic tables and chairs self-service cafeteria. As soon as you stepped into the dining saloon your shoes sank into thick carpets. Tablecloths as thick as blankets covered the tables. The plates were heavy and did not move around the tables very easily. The knives and forks were so heavy that it was very difficult for a blind person to tell whether or not there was any food on the end of the fork. Apart from dining with Captain Jack, I believe this was the only time I had actually dined in the dining saloon. The waiter came offering soup, which we accepted. He came with the main course - roast beef, Yorkshire pudding and whatever, which we accepted. The pudding duly came followed by the bill, which was thirteen shillings each. As I fumbled about trying to find an extra copper or two, Kev had already legged it off to Mother, sleeping down below in one of the lounges, for the extra cash to meet our shortfall. We went the rest of the day absolutely broke and if it hadn't been for Aunt Kathleen buying us a football each in one of Dublin's shops, we would have returned to the Island empty handed.

Returning to St Vincent's after the Easter holidays of 1969 was a slightly different experience from usual. For the first time in eleven years, part of me was actually looking forward to going back, because this was to be my last three months at school. The end was in sight and the sooner things got started the better. Before long I would be just like my older brother, Lenny, working and bringing in cash. Where I would find work on the Island had not crossed my mind, I thought only of how I would be coming home forever, and of how the lonely beaches and quiet streets of Castletown would be mine for the rest of my life. Just three short months lay between the realization of this dream and me. Some kind of college training had been mentioned at school, but I had paid little heed to this. I was hell-bent on leaving school and returning home as soon as possible, and nothing was going to get in the way of that.

The last term at St Vincent's passed fairly uneventfully. Of course, it dragged on and on as if it would never end. I got the usual half dozen cautions for smoking and several reprimands for play acting and practical jokes. I did now have one or two luxuries such as a bottle of tomato sauce. The school dinners were still the usual meat, boiled spuds and a veg. The school did not provide any kind of sauce, but by now they did not object to me bringing in a bottle of my own. It's amazing what difference a simple bottle of tomato sauce can make to a plain and boring meal.

I would sit no exams as I was on route one to freedom. Nonetheless, it was decided that I should travel down to Birmingham to the Queen Alexandra College of Engineering, in the hope that I might secure a place there. My chances of pulling this off were rated as pretty remote as it was thought the college would be somewhat reluctant to take on a student who did not even have something as basic as a G.C.S.E. exam to his name. However, the interview was duly arranged and Mother travelled over from the Island to accompany me down to Birmingham. I was really just going through the motions with this, as from what I had heard from the staff at school, I didn't have a chance. Just before I left for Birmingham, Sister Claire took me into her office and gave me all the tips she could think of in a desperate last-ditch bid to help obtain me a place there. I remember feeling really grateful to her and I felt that I had let her down; she had given me so much over the years and this was no way to repay her.

Sitting on the train on the way down to Birmingham I felt as though I had let everyone down, teachers, nuns, Mum and Dad, the lot. I was leaving school, and after eleven years I was leaving with nothing. In a bid to get home as quickly as possible I had thrown everything away. Sure, I would be back home but with no tools to enable me to stay there. I was heading at 70 miles an hour towards a college which wouldn't want to know me, and without their help I would not be qualified to hold down a job anywhere. "Oh, dear God, please help me!" I felt then rather two-faced asking God for His help after disowning Him for the last eleven years. If He was out there, why should He help me now? I cheered up with the thought that at least the college had granted me an interview, and they wouldn't be doing that if there weren't a chance of a start there. Maybe the somewhat despondent prayer I had uttered was starting to be answered.

We reached Birmingham and made our way out to the college on the number 3 bus. Harbourne, the district of Birmingham where the college was situated, was about six miles from the railway station, about the same distance as St Vincent's was from the Pier Head. It was almost as if I was starting all over again. On our arrival at the college, Mother and I were led into a small room, together with a few other folks who had come for the same reason. We sat there for what seemed like a lifetime as the others filed into the interview room. At last, they called my name out and I shuffled my way into the office that was about to seal my fate.

Mr Cannon, the college principle, was a quietly-spoken, gentle man. "So, Thomas, you have come all the way from the Isle of Man and you would like to come and join us, eh?" "Yes," I replied. "And you would like to take up engineering as a career, eh? "Yes, I would, Sir." "Did you not think it would be a good idea to stay on at school and obtain some qualifications then?" "Well, I would like to get on with it as soon as possible, I guess." That was about the best I could manage. He must have thought that I was really keen. At least, that's what I hoped for. To my astonishment my interview all but came to an end at this point. Mr Cannon suggested that I would only be wasting time staying on at school if it was engineering I wanted, and suggested that I come and join the college in September. Just a few short months away. I was beside myself with excitement. My interview was over in about five minutes flat and, more importantly, I was in! There must be a God after all. I had not found Him in the chapel at St Vincent's but He had turned up here at the Queen Alexandra College in Birmingham. My mother and I walked from Mr Cannon's office and an hour or two later we were back on the train making our way back to Liverpool. I had a smile on my face and an ego as big as the planet! For once, my name was read out at school assembly the next morning, not to tell me to stand outside Sister Claire's office, but for my achievement. I think I had to hold myself down in my seat, as usually when my name was read out, I simply started walking. Now I could leave school in style and go home at the end of term with my head held high. I was not a complete failure and I was going somewhere even if I wasn't quite sure where at this stage.

The last few weeks of that school term seem to take an age to pass but pass they did. It was customary for the school to throw a party for school leavers on the last night of school. It was July 1969, and on the day I was leaving school Neil Armstrong was landing on the moon. The wildest dreams were coming true. The telly being turned on to watch the moon landing interrupted our party, I had followed Armstrong's progress with great interest but his finale had coincided with mine. He might be landing on the moon but I was leaving Liverpool and going home to Castletown. Well done, Neil, mate, but simply nothing was going to overshadow my big day. I don't think I slept a wink on that final night. It was unbelievable that it was all over. I pushed the college and Birmingham from my mind. That was simply nothing more than a blur on my horizon. There would be no more good-byes, no more tears, nor more grief. I had served my time and, just like a captive bird, I would soon be released to fly freely across the open sky. Of course, the good-byes were not quite over, there would be plenty of good-byes tomorrow but not painful ones. They would simply be good-bye and thank you to the nuns, teachers and fellow pupils. I just might, for the first time, actually enjoy saying good-bye. That would be a new experience.

I was lying awake waiting for Sister Cissy when she turned up bang on cue with her morning call. I had been woken up now thousands of times to that by now so familiar, "Time to get up, boys." I was going to savour every moment of today. I would listen out for every bell, walk every corridor and even try to enjoy my last two meals. I had specially asked to be allowed to sail home on my last day. I wanted to sail down the Mersey just as I had sailed up it eleven years ago and this had been granted. Although this was a huge occasion for me and probably for the six other pupils who were leaving on this day, for the rest of the school it was just another going-home day. As the day wore on, my wild excitement became tempered by what I thought would be little more than routine events. Saying good-bye was not going to be just a run-of-the-mill affair. These nuns and teachers had been part of my life both in class and at play for eleven years, and now it was time to part. It had not crossed my mind that I would miss them, that a kind of bonding had taken place. Until now they had been my disciplinarians, my teachers, my substitute parents. It had certainly never occurred to me that they loved me or were fond of me; and, even more extraordinarily, I was discovering that I was fond of them, too. They had cared for me up until now and they cared about what would happen to me in the future. I was not going to be simply jumping with delight when I walked down that drive, a part of me, just a little part, was still clinging to St Vincent's and would have to be gently prised away.

When I arrived at the main hall with most of my good-byes said, there was just enough time for one last forgotten task. I turned and walked down the long corridor, and stopped at the porch of the school chapel. I removed from my pocket two half crowns and placed them in the holy souls' collection box. This would by no means cover my debt to the holy souls, but I could now leave with a slightly easier conscience. I made my way back to the front door and I was just a little bit disappointed to find that Mr Allen, a teacher of whom I was very fond and to whom I owed a great deal, had brought the car round to the front door. I had intended to walk down that long gravel drive just as I had walked up it eleven years earlier. However, I was not going to argue, after all he was taking me to the boat, so instead I settled for listening to the tyres of the car crunching on the gravel as we slowly rolled to the end of the drive. It was almost over too quickly. With a left turn, the sound of crunching gravel gave way to the noiseless, smooth, tarmac road. We were on our way to the Pier Head and St Vincent's was history.

As I sat in the lounge of the *Manx Maid,* waiting for her to pull away from the landing stage, my mind drifted back over the last eleven years. I had planned probably hundreds of escapes but only a few got past the planning stage. I had actually made three attempts to get away, but only managed once to get outside the school. I remembered how one summer evening I found myself wandering across the school playing field. For some reason, a severe attack of homesickness came upon me and I just kept walking, down the drive and out on to the road, where I stood at the bus stop, then boarded a bus for the Pier Head. I don't remember why, but for some reason the bus terminated in the city a mile or so from the Pier Head. I left the bus and headed for the Isle of Man ferry. I doubt I would have had enough for the boat fare and there probably wasn't even a boat due to sail anyway. I remember hearing voices coming from inside a pub en route. As I stumbled along on the pavement, probably very much regretting my actions, a man with a scouse accent befriended me. "Whare ya goin', laa?" "To the Isle of Man boat," I replied." "Cum on, laa, you're from the blind school out in West Derby, I just happen to be going that way so I'll drop yer off there and no one will ever know any different. I won't even come in with yer, just drop yer at the drive way." He was true to his word and no one ever knew of my abortive attempt at escaping.

As I sat there in the lounge reminiscing over my years in Liverpool, I noticed the vibration under my feet which meant we were pulling away from the landing stage and heading out into the river. I had sailed up this same river in 1958 as a small child full of fear of the unknown and with eyes filled with tears. Now in 1969 I was sailing back down the river as a young man and returning home with mission accomplished and with tears, too, but this time tears of joy. I knew the river extremely well and could tell where we were by my Braille watch. At fifteen minutes into the voyage we passed New Brighton. I remembered all the wonderful days I had had there, either on school outings or sailing over on the ferryboat with my school chums at weekends. Then on to Moreton, leaving the Wirral peninsula behind us on the port side, the river now widening to embrace the River Dee, and beyond that the coast of North Wales. As we passed Crosby on our starboard side, I thought of George Spears, who had been my teacher for the last couple of years. I also thought of him as a friend. He lived in Crosby and before becoming a teacher he had been a radio officer for many years, including the war years. Each morning before class started, he had filled me in with what was going on on the river, which he could see from his house. I would miss George. After about thirty-five minutes we passed Formby, again on the starboard side; and then we were past the Mersey Bar and into the Irish Sea. It would be four hours before anyone saw land again, and then it would be my beloved homeland, Ellan Vannin

I guess that passage in July 1969 was just another everyday voyage for the crew of the *Manx Maid* but for me it was one of those very special days that only come along once or twice in a lifetime; they pass by all too soon and, of course, can never be recaptured.

Chapter Eighteen

The summer holiday of 1969 passed by much as any other had done except that I was now spending a lot more time fishing with my friend and neighbour, Michael Quine, than mucking about with my mates. Michael had left the Steam Packet Company and was fishing full time out of the hamlet of Derbyhaven. I knew I was going to miss the fishing when I went to college. I had always harboured hopes that I would go to sea as soon as I left school, and even though it had been explained to me a thousand times that it was impossible, the flame of hope had always burned inside me. In truth, I don't think it ever really went out. It remained smouldering away inside me even through college, and when I sailed with Michael it burst into flames.

Michael's boat was a small, 16-foot, clinker-built vessel with a five horse power outboard Seagull engine. He fished for lobsters while I played an active part aboard the boat, baiting and hauling lobster-pots, and even steering the boat using the wind as a guide. Michael would set my course by telling me to keep the wind on the left side of my face, and thus he would be free to attend to other tasks. The lobsters were caught in baited pots that were made from a steel frame covered in netting. At the top of the pot was a plastic, tapered tunnel, usually made from a plant pot with the bottom burned out of it. On the inside of the pot, placed at the narrow end of the tunnel, was a wire with a fish-head hanging from it. The lobster would swim into the pot though the wide end of the tunnel and then be unable to negotiate the narrow exit to swim out again. There was also the landing of the lobsters. Once the pots had been hauled aboard, the lobsters would have to be removed. A lobster is more than capable of chopping your finger off with its powerful nippers, so these would have to be secured with elastic bands. Holding the lobster firmly between your knees with a tight grip on one nipper, you threaded an elastic band tightly round the other until until the lobster could not open it. Once you had banded the first nipper, you simply turned the lobster about and banded the second one. I learned all these tasks sailing on the *Siesta,* which was the name of Michael's little craft, and I was going to miss sailing on the *Siesta* terribly when the time came to go Birmingham.

In a way my dream of being a fisherman had come true, in as much as Michael was paying me. I was at sea but I wasn't going to risk telling Dad, Mum and the education authorities that I had found a job and would not be attending college now after all though I must admit is was sorely tempting. Apart from my Dad, Michael was the only person who gave me real hope. Yes, I had been given all the usual assurances from the professionals - teachers, nuns and career advisers. But I didn't really want to be an engineer, a piano tuner or a basket maker. They were the traditional occupations that blind people took up. I wanted to be at sea and when I was with Michael I was fulfilling this dream. Michael never told me what I couldn't do. He didn't mind and would allow me to take on any task at all on board the *Siesta.* My blindness made no difference whatsoever to his attitude towards me, sometimes to his cost, as I am sure he was often the butt of jokes by the other fishermen. After all, I doubt that there were ever any other fishing boats that had a blind crewman aboard. He took all this in his stride and was never deterred by the thoughts or actions of others. He always had time to teach and never answered questions with answers such as, "because that's the way we do it", or, "just do as you're told". There would always be a considered and well thought out answer to all my numerous questions.

I was never more happy and content than when I was sailing with Michael, for this was my true vocation. When at sea on the *Siesta,* I was a king on his throne, a bird on the wing. This was where I belonged. I don't know why it should have been considered so unusual for me to want to go to sea, for a large proportion of our community earned their living from the sea. It was inherent in islanders and, after all, that's what I was. Blind I may be, but my instincts were no different from anyone else's, and the pull of the sea had just as vice-like a grip on me as it had on anyone else. However, college and Birmingham beckoned and come what may that's where I was bound. I decided that I would go through the motions and then return and take up my place on the *Siesta* with Michael.

I suppose the major difference at the end of the summer holiday of 1969 was that, come late August, I didn't get that awful feeling that used to well up inside me about a week before I was due to return to St Vincent's. Of course, I was only too aware that come September I would be off once again, but this was different. This time I knew that if I really didn't want to head off to college in Birmingham there wasn't a lot anyone could do to make me. In reality, I knew that I had to go - but it made me feel a little better just thinking that the choice was mine. The situation was further eased by the fact that I had two uncles and two aunts - my dad's sister, Trudy, and her husband, Norman, and my dad's brother, Reg, and his wife, Val. They all lived in Coventry, a city only about 18 miles from Birmingham, which meant that I could get away from College and be a week-ender.

Chapter Nineteen

In my school days the first cold breezes of going back to school had started to blow when Mother began shopping for my college clothes. This time, instead of shopping for a school uniform she went shopping for boiler suits and working clothes, as stipulated on the list sent to us by the college. I would need clothes that were intended to become oily and dirty. This made me feel better and I was now sixteen years old, and more in control of my emotions than when I was a child at St Vincent's.

Arriving in Liverpool was not quite the same on my trips to Birmingham. For one thing I hadn't actually arrived anywhere yet. Liverpool was now only the half-way point of my journey. I had a train to catch which left Lime Street Station at 1.28 p.m. Providing the boat was punctual, this allowed me just 28 minutes to get from the Pier Head to the station. Most of the time I was lucky and had met someone on board who was continuing by train after the boat had docked. Otherwise I had to try and persuade reluctant Liverpool taxi drivers to take me to the station. The drivers were not too keen on taking an unaccompanied blind chap to a railway station as they could not leave their cab, and I guess they would have felt a little guilty at simply chucking me out at the station and leaving me to my own devices. When this occurred, I would stand around on the taxi rank waiting for someone to be heading in my direction and then tag along with them. I was often helped by the crew of the Steam Packet ship, who would seek out someone intending to travel to Birmingham, or at least to the railway station. Sometimes, if no one could be found, one of the crew would come all the way with me.

I was met in Birmingham's New Street Station by a member of the college staff, as was the custom for new students. My arrival at the Queen Alexandra College was not as dramatic or emotional as my first day at St Vincent's. I had kidded myself that I was here of my own choice and I suppose that took care of the emotional side of it. After a short tour around the building, I was left pretty much to myself. There were no big dormitories and I would share a room with two others - Steve, a likeable, chirpy cockney and Malcolm, a brash and down-to-earth Mancunian. There was a students lounge where I was free to smoke if I wished, although I must say it did feel a little strange at first lighting up a cigarette in front of one of the teachers. I soon got used to it. There was a dining room, but no one cared very much whether you turned up for meals or not. You went to bed whenever you liked and you got up in the mornings without being called by any of the staff. You were free to come and go from the college whenever you liked outside of study hours and if you didn't like the college's evening meal, well, there was a chippy just down the road. On top of this, I was to receive 15 shillings a week from the college, which I was free to spend down the pub, on fags or whatever I wanted. It was also good to see that two of my old school mates, Bob Dysart from Blackburn and Noel from County Armagh, were also at the College. This was not going to be a bad place at all. My first phone call home was a positive one.

I was not to go straight into the engineering shop. For the first three months I would be assessed, and after that, if it were deemed that I was suitable, I would start in the engineering shop the following term. I spent the first term taking old telephones to bits and putting all the various parts in boxes, assembling small door catches and chopping firewood for the elderly residents of Harbourne. Well, it was better than lessons and by and large I enjoyed it. I was also given mobility lessons with a long cane. Up until now I had never really used a white stick as it always seemed to me that carrying a white stick around was a bit like wearing a badge telling everyone I was blind. I wanted as much as possible to be treated in exactly the same way as anyone else by the general public, so I had avoided white sticks and dark glasses and up until now had got by pretty well. However, if I wanted to roam around Birmingham on my own, I had no choice but to learn how to use the long cane and somewhat reluctantly took it up.

Although I had so much more freedom in Birmingham than I had known in Liverpool, Birmingham was a different kettle of fish altogether. As far as I could tell, it had no beginning, and no end. There was no seawater, for one thing, no docks, no Pier Head, just lots and lots of traffic, streets and houses. You could travel on a bus for hours and not go anywhere. When you got off the bus there was simply more of the same. More houses, more streets, more traffic. It just did not end. When you got off the train at the station you were slap bang in the middle of it all and that's exactly where you stayed no matter where you went, the sprawling mass of the big city went with you. This was no place for a seafaring man such as me. At least Liverpool started somewhere, at the docks. It had a river, its people by and large knew the sea and had seafaring stories to tell. Here, talking of the sea was as if you were talking a foreign language. They had never even heard of the Isle of Man. I felt much further away from home than I had ever felt before, even though I had my uncles and aunts to visit at week-ends. I got the feeling that even the birds that sang from the roof tops were only here because they knew no better.

One of the few things that I had going for me in the big cities was football, but Villa Park was a far cry from Anfield, and I did not become hypnotised by Villa Park in the way that I had been by Anfield. Aston Villa were then in the second division and I only went there once. I felt sorry for the crowd and wished I could pick them up and transport them to Anfield so that they could enjoy the atmosphere and experience the sense of humour of the Kop. I don't even remember who the Villa were playing on the one and only match I attended, it really was a totally insignificant occasion. I remember wondering if the pitch they were playing on was the only bit of greenery in the whole of Birmingham. I did actually return to Villa Park later, but not to attend a match. The manager at the time, Tommy Docherty, invited several of us students from the college to a lunch hosted by himself at Villa Park. The club sacked him on the same day but to his credit, even though he must have known his fate, he continued with the lunch and showed us around the ground without showing the slightest sign of frustration.

With my first week behind me, I headed off to spend the week-end with my Uncle Norman, known to the family as Normie, and Auntie Trudy. They lived up in the sky, on the eleventh floor of a high-rise block of flats in Coventry. I decided to travel to Coventry on a Midland Red bus as it was cheaper than the train. I boarded the number 3 bus that stopped right outside the college and took me straight into Birmingham city centre. I tapped my way down Corporation Street with my new white long cane. In order to get to the Midland Red bus station, it was necessary to negotiate the concourse above New Street railway station. This was a battle I was to engage in twice a week and frequently lost. However, it was a necessary evil if I wanted to spend my week-ends in Coventry. On the first occasion I recall being totally lost. I was thrashing about with my cane amongst crowds of people who were all hurrying and scurrying about, going to their various destinations, when an Indian or Pakistani voice boomed out from within them: "Left! Right! Straight ahead!." He kept this up, walking just behind me, without knowing where I was going, all the way through the concourse. It was as if I was out on some sort of army leave with the sergeant major trailing behind me, barking his instructions as we wended our way through the busy Friday evening rush-hour crowds in the railway station.

With the help of my somewhat forthright guide I duly arrived at the Midland Red bus station, and after parting with four and eight-pence, I was soon roaring my way to Coventry. Riding on the Midland Red bus was a totally different experience from that of meandering along on the Castletown to Douglas bus. The driver seemed to brake only at the last minute when approaching a stop, sending tumbling folks who were standing in the aisle preparing to leave the bus. The same procedure seemed to apply to those who were boarding the bus. No one was given time to take their seats, for as soon as they had parted with their cash we were on our way and flailing arms grabbed you as the passenger lunged at every seat along the way to prevent themselves from hurtling down the bus. It was certainly a far cry from back home on the Island where the driver not only seemed to know everyone he picked up, but would often have a personal chat with them before they sat down and always appeared to have all the time in the world to do so.

My week-ends in Coventry were to alternate between uncles. One week I would stay with Normie and Trudy in their Cross Street flat.

The next week I would stay with Uncle Reg and Auntie Val on the other side of town in Ivy Walk. There was quite a contrast between the two. Normie and Trudy, up in the sky in the city centre, and Reg and Val out in the suburbs. The social side of staying in the two places was quite a contrast as well. A night out with Normie was likely to be spent in a city-centre pub where anything went, whereas a typical night out with Reg was likely to be spent in a working men's club. Uncle Reg was a great favourite in the clubs as he was a first class yodeller and no Saturday night in the Colliery Club was complete without his Slim-Whitman-style renditions of "China Doll", "The Old Cattle Call", and so on. I continued to alternate between my two uncles' abodes until Normie and Trudy decided to up sticks and return to the Isle of Man. Dad had now left the Gas Works and he and Normie were to form a partnership and go in for landscape gardening. Of course, I still had Uncle Reg and Auntie Val for my weekends but Normie and Trudy had not left Coventry without providing for me; from now on I was to spend every other week-end with Normie's mother, Dolly.

Dolly lived close to the city centre with her son, Normie's brother, Terry. In 1970 there was very little in the way of work in Coventry. Dolly's husband had died some years earlier. She now scraped along from day to day making do with whatever she had, and the little she had she would often part with to someone else whose need she deemed was greater, something she usually found to be the case. I frequently arrived on a Friday evening broke. As Terry and myself sat in front of the telly, cigaretteless and penniless, Dolly would wander off upstairs. After a few minutes, she would return having scraped together ten shillings or so, handing it over to Terry and insisting that he take himself and me over the road to The Jolly Roger. I recall her apologising one Friday night for only being able to serve up a plate of chips and sausages, when she had made do with just a plate of chips for herself so that there would be enough sausages to go round for us. She was indeed a dear, kind soul who would freely give you whatever she had, and would derive more pleasure from what her last shilling might do for you, than what it may have done for her. Eventually, Dolly followed Normie and Trudy over to the Isle of Man and ended her days there.

My relations in Coventry were now thinning out; there was only

Uncle Reg and Auntie Val left. However, I continued to commute between Birmingham and Coventry spending every week-end with them. There were one or two hairy incidents whilst I was en route between the two cities. On one occasion, whilst making my way along Corporation Street in Birmingham one Sunday night to return to college, I pulled out my wallet from my back pocket so that I would have my bus pass at the ready for boarding the number 3 bus. As I thumbed through it trying to locate my pass, it was suddenly snatched from my hands. As I stood there in disbelief clutching at the Birmingham night air, a voice suddenly announced, "Can I help?" "Who are you?" I asked. "I'm a police officer," said the voice. "And how do I know you are a police officer?" I replied. I had by now learned not to be quite so trusting of everyone I might meet in the city centre, particularly at night-time. He muttered something into his radio about being with a blind gentleman and would the voice at the other end please confirm his status. Of course, they did. I explained about my wallet and that there was nothing in it apart from my bus pass, and he took down my name and details with the enthusiasm of someone who believed that they might actually find it. He continued along the street with me and waited for the number 3 bus to arrive. When it did, he explained my predicament to the driver. I continued with my free bus ride back to the college. The next morning a police car turned up at the college and my wallet was handed back to me. Obviously it had been discarded by the thief and handed into a police station. My confidence in walking the city centre had taken a bit of a blow with the loss of my wallet, but the actions of the Birmingham police certainly went a long way to establishing my faith in the guardians of the city.

On that occasion I was the injured party, but there was another time when I actually was the perpetrator of a mugging. It took place on the same street and on another Sunday evening on my way back from Coventry. There was an Irish guy, and although I didn't know him, I referred to him as Paddy. Paddy used to sell baked spuds from a wheel barrow on Corporation Street. He must have had some kind of little stove mounted on his barrow or cart. One night, as I tapped my way down the street with my long cane, Paddy must have had his back to me and I ploughed straight into his barrow, knocking it, the spuds and his stove all over the street. I certainly must have deprived

111

him of a night's takings at least. I do not recall meeting up with Paddy again, so I take this opportunity to apologise to him, and hope that now some thirty years on he can find it in his heart to forgive me.

My first three months assessment term passed over quickly. I was deemed by those in power to be of suitable material for the engineering shop and I began my second term on the shop floor. I was taught how to read micrometers and so on, and learned what words such as thermal conductivity and ductivity meant. I won't bore you with the meanings or brag that I still remember them. By and large, I enjoyed the work in the engineering shop, but despite this, and the fact that I went off to Coventry for my week-ends, for some inexplicable reason I was homesick here, as much, if not more, than I had been at St Vincent's. We still had no phone at home and in order to speak with Dad I would telephone our local pub, The Duck's Nest, from time to time. It didn't really matter whether he would be in there or not, as I knew that whoever answered the phone would pass a message on. I became reluctant to make these calls, as just hearing the voices in the background in The Duck's Nest triggered off my homesickness.

My biggest low in the two years I was at the college came whilst I was travelling home one half-term. In order to get home, I had to catch a train from Birmingham that would get me into Liverpool in time for the 11 a.m. boat to Douglas. This meant catching a bus at about 7 a.m. from the college to connect with a train that departed around half-seven. I have always been a cautious sort of guy and would always be at the station or dockside long before the train or boat was due to go. This time, as I sat on the bus on my way to Birmingham Railway Station, I discovered that I had left the college without my train and boat tickets. I immediately made my way down to the front of the bus and explained my situation to the driver. I think he might have spotted a tear in my eye, as the thought dawned on me that I might be about to spend my half-term holiday in Birmingham. He could not have been more helpful as he stopped the bus at the next stop and walked across the road with me to the bus stop for the buses going back to college. "There will be a bus along in about five minutes," he explained. After doing a quick calculation, he worked out that if all went well and I could find my tickets quickly, I would just about make the train. As we parted he asked if I would give the bus station a ring if I made it home, as he would be thinking of me. The bus back to college came soon enough and I think if it had been an Olympic event, I would have been a gold medal holder for running with the white stick over a hundred-yard dash, up several flights of stairs and back. I made it back to the station with a couple of minutes to spare. I did not need to make the phone call to the first bus driver, as the bus that was now carrying me pulled in right outside the station. The driver explained to me that his mate had explained everything to him and between them they had arranged for a member of staff from the railway station to meet the bus and hurry me to the train. Indeed, the folks of Birmingham were every bit as good as any I have met.

There was more travelling time now needed between Birmingham and the Island; it was not simply a matter of jumping on a boat at Liverpool. Just as at school, the college term always ended at lunchtime on the last day. This meant that I missed the 11 a.m. sailing from Liverpool, and in wintertime I would not be able to pick up a sailing until the next day, causing me to lose a day's holiday. In the summer time there would be an afternoon ferry sailing at 3.30 that would get me into Douglas at 7.30. Too late for a man who was eager to savour every minute of his holiday. I recall the end of one such summer term when I sauntered along to the principal's office to ask Mr Cannon if I could begin my end-of-term release first thing in the morning as my boat sailed from Liverpool at 11 a.m. I omitted to tell him that there was another at 3.30. I guessed he would not check up on this, and I took full advantage of his ignorance of the sea. "I suppose the boat has to sail in accordance with the tides?" he asked. "Yes, Sir," I replied, trying to mask my excitement. There were no seafaring folks down here and now this was to my advantage. If Mr Cannon had been a nautical man, he would have known that the port of Liverpool was a deep water port and that even at low tide there was enough water there to float the Queen Mary. On the way home I pondered that surely Mr Cannon would twig on eventually and question why, if my boat depended on the tides, did it sail at 11 a.m. every time I was due to go home. Fortunately, he never did. Time again for an apology.

Chapter Twenty

Virtually all of my holiday at home was now spent on the *Siesta* with Michael. I still harboured the idea that one day I would go to sea. Even at college, with the foundations of a career in engineering being laid, I still had not completely given up this notion. And if I couldn't actually physically go to sea, well maybe there was a chance of gaining a shore job with the Steam Packet. This proved to be another dream that remained unfulfilled. But for now, sailing with Michael was the dream becoming reality. It wasn't inconceivable that, when college was over and after I had held down a job in some factory or other, I could leave and go and join Michael on the *Siesta*. It wasn't just a pipe dream, for Michael was more than willing to have me as a crew-member even though he knew of the flack he would receive from Dad, and, of course, the authorities. Well, as things panned out, this turned out to be yet another unfulfilled dream, though this one came much closer than the previous two.

Putting to sea on the *Siesta* during my holidays from college was a truly magical feeling. Because she was such a small craft, only 16 feet in length and 4 foot 6 inches wide, you felt every motion. We danced with and over the big breakers when the weather was hostile and gently lolloped up and down with the tide on calm summer days. The sea becomes totally addictive in the same way that smoking or anything else does. I could hear and understand what everyone was saying to me about not being able to go to sea for a career, but at the same time, it had a pull on me like nothing else I have ever experi-

Sunrise over Derbyhaven. Nothing gave the author greater pleasure than an early morning visit to Derbyhaven with its familiar sounds and the prospect of a day's fishing along the coast.

enced. I knew that when I was at sea with Michael, I was happy, doing the only thing I really wanted to do. What drives a man back to sea when, at the end of a winter's day's fishing, after the waves have broken over the sides of the boat and been so cold they have been like slabs of stone smashing into him, and his fingers and toes are so numb he has lost his sense of touch in them, and the pain in his ears tells him that they have had enough of the cold sea air, he climbs on to the quayside and says to himself, "That's it, no more for me." Yet the next morning you rise again at four or five o'clock and start the whole procedure all over again, just as if the previous day had never happened.

During my sea-going days with Michael we had many memorable trips; indeed there were a few where Lady Luck and maybe God smiled on us, but then that's just part and parcel of going to sea. There was one trip in particular with Michael that I will always remember, although at the time it would have been a trip no different from any other as far as he was concerned. It was the last day of my holidays and we left the tiny sea port of Derbyhaven on the early morning tide. I always loved sailing out of Derbyhaven, especially on a fine summer morning with just enough breeze for the little *Siesta* to waltz to. It was one of those beautiful mornings, the kind that makes you feel good to be alive. Of course, you tend to take even more notice than normal when you know that tomorrow you have to be away and it would be months before you would get the chance again. As we hugged the coastline on our way north, hauling pots as we sailed, I could hear the gulls calling further out to sea from the starboard side. From the port side, I could hear the sound of the jackdaws coming from the shore. With the waves gently breaking on the rocks, it was almost as if the sea and her friends were giving me a musical send off, and the little *Siesta* seemed to be dancing to their tune. With tomorrow looming, I could not believe that I would just sail away and give all this up. The very idea that I would swap this idyllic scene for the mad rush of Birmingham seemed unimaginable. When we returned to Derbyhaven later that day, I remember walking up the little slipway and standing on the roadside. There was not a single car in sight, not even the hum of any distant traffic. The only sound to be heard was coming from the oyster-catchers further over on the beach, and the noise of Michael's boots crunching through the shingle as he secured the *Siesta* to a mooring. My spirits fell to my boots as I imagined the head-splitting noise of the big city that I was about to trade all this for.

I duly crossed to Liverpool on the Steam Packet steamer the next day and as I sat on the train wending my way towards Birmingham, I knew it was worse this time. This time the homesickness was not just a horrible gut feeling, it was painful. As I sat on the number 3 bus making my way through Birmingham's busy city centre, my thoughts drifted back to Michael, who would now be sailing back to Derbyhaven having completed his day's work. Amongst the crowds of passengers pushing and shoving to get on and off the bus, two women got on and sat beside me. The bus was full of passengers and the air was full of the sound of their city voices all talking frantically. I just couldn't stand it any longer and burst into tears. The two women, who I guess were taken by surprise at my outburst, tried to console me, but, of course, I pulled myself together pretty quickly. I'm sure I didn't tell them the truth about my outburst, but I can't actually remember what story I placated them with. It would have been obvious to them where I was going as the bus stopped right outside the college. I felt stupid and hoped that they would not make any enquiries asking how I was. Fortunately they never did, and another term at the Queen Alexandra College got under way.

With my Uncle Normie, Auntie Trudy and Normie's mother, Dolly, now all back on the Isle of Man, I continued to visit Uncle Reg and Auntie Val in Coventry at week-ends. Now and again I would take a trip a bit further to St Albans in Hertfordshire to visit my dad's other brother, Uncle Arthur, and his wife, Pam. Arthur had left the Island some thirty years earlier and had done well as a builder down there. I sometimes wondered how it was that my dad's brothers, Reg and Arthur, and my mother's brothers, Louis, Sean and Tommy, had all managed to leave home without it bothering them, seeming to be just as happy elsewhere. I never did and still don't know the answer to this conundrum. I only know that I loved home and would not be happy and would not rest until such time that I returned there for good.

During this term, it occurred to me to simply catch a train running in the opposite direction one Friday night, one that was going north to Liverpool as opposed to south to Coventry, jump on a boat and simply return home and take my chances. I didn't do it, for whatever reason. However, at the end of that term I decided I had finally had enough and would return home for good. I had the basics in engineering skills and reckoned I knew enough to hold down a fairly junior job in some factory or other. I did not tell the college of my decision in case they tried to talk me out of it. Also, by saying nothing, I left the door open should I bottle out during the holidays. I did not bottle out, although I left it until about three days before I was due to return, before I told Dad and Mother of my decision. The response from them was all too predictable: I would not be able to get a job. What about all the training I had been through so far, was I going to just waste it? I would soon tire of being home all the time and find that it was probably not the wonderful life I seemed to think it was. Without a job, without any money, home would soon lose its appeal. I wasn't unduly concerned, after all, if I didn't get a job, then sooner or later I would end up with Michael on the *Siesta,* and although that would get me a lot of stick, at the end of the day, that was what I really wanted, anyway.

Chapter Twenty-one

I was not exactly brimming with confidence on the day I found myself standing in the office of Graham Pidcock, then the Island's youth employment officer. My mother had made the trip into Douglas with me and amidst several "I told you so's" from her, I related my situation to Graham. In 1971, there were not too many blind people on the Island, and I didn't know of any with a job in engineering. It was going to be extremely difficult, but Mr Pidcock promised that he would do his best. He requested that we left him for an hour or so while he made some phone calls and return later. Of course, we obliged and returned to his office an hour or so later. On my return, he informed me that he had managed to persuade a firm called Davis Charlton, which made model aircraft and boat engines, to give me an interview, and that if I would go there now they would give me an interview immediately. Needless to say, I could not get down to Hills Meadow, which was where the factory was located, quickly enough.

On arriving at the factory I was ushered into an office where Mr Hefin Davis, the owner of the factory, was sitting waiting for me. I could tell by the murmuring of the staff that it was a bit unusual for Mr Davis himself to carry out an interview for a job. I kept nothing from him. I simply told him my story of Birmingham and that I had now been away from home for about thirteen years and I simply just wanted to return. I would do any kind of a job and even work for nothing for a few weeks and, if they didn't like me or I didn't come up to scratch, I could simply leave and that would be that. "There will

118

be no need for that, boyo," he replied in his rich South Wales accent. "I can well understand that you want to come home and I will do my best to accommodate you." I couldn't believe what I was hearing. It was like I had died and gone to Heaven. He picked up the phone and summoned one of his foremen up to his office. "Now then, Jim," he began, "this is Tom and he is joining us on Monday morning." "Good God, to do what?" said the foreman. "He will work on the honing machines," said Mr Davis. The cylinders and pistons in a model air-craft engine are very small and the inside of the tiny cylinder has to be ground out using a very fine grinding stone. Then, by pushing the piston up the cylinder with your finger placed firmly over the top, you could test the compression. "We are going to put this young man's very keen sense of touch to use," said Mr Davis. "He is totally blind and will have a keener sense of touch than you and your gang down there in the fitting shop." I could tell the foreman was used to doing what he was told, as he offered no more than a deep sigh to this totally unexpected instruction he had been given.

I walked out of that office the happiest guy on the Isle of Man. I hadn't even asked how much I would be paid. I didn't know the first thing about the job I was about to take up, but I was home now and this time for good. It really was all over. I had been through the mill, crawled over the broken glass, but this was the reward. I was home forever. I had won the lottery and the football pools and had had about fifty Christmases all in the space of about half an hour. I don't think I said, "I told you so!" to my mother, but it was breaking my rib cage to say so.

As soon as I got home I phoned Graham Pidcock and thanked him for playing his part in my being given the greatest gift anyone could ever present me with. Then, of course, the college had to be told and, naturally, everyone in Castletown would have to know that this time I was home for good. However, within a few months my mother had more to worry about than me and my newly-born career. There was another new-born on the way, in the shape of my youngest brother, Sean. I think this late family arrival was a bigger shock than my somewhat premature employment and Sean's arrival helped to take the pressure off me, at any rate at home, as he diverted the attention of both my Mother and my Father away from me.

Davis Charlton had a 7.45 a.m. start. A strange time to start work, but then, as I was to learn, Mr Hefin Davis was a strange kind of guy. The firm was divided into two parts - the engine section, which was the section that concentrated on the model engines, and what we called the big factory, which made parts for the Rolls Royce Company. On my first day I was given a box of tiny engine-cylinders and pistons, briefly shown what to do and then sort of left to get on with it. Of course, I made a complete mess of the job. In Birmingham I had been taught to work within tolerances of two thousands of an inch. Here the tolerances were two tenths of one thousandth of an inch. My Braille micrometer could read these extreme tolerances but it was pushing it to its absolute limits. My nearest workmate, who worked on the machine next to me most of the time doing the same job, was a likeable Yorkshireman by the name of Arthur. Arthur took me under his wing, and with his careful guidance I began to learn the knack of honing. Mr Davis decided to pay me exactly the same as the other apprentices and more or less treated me the same as he did them.

I remember standing at the bus stop in Douglas with my first week's wages. This was what it was all about, this had been what all the sacrifices had been for. All the tears, goodbyes and heartbreak. They had all happened so that one day I would hold this envelope in my hand. It seemed a hell of a price to pay for such a small envelope. I wanted to keep it and plonk it on the table in front of Mother and let her open it, but I couldn't. I had given everything for this thing. I would open it now, here at the bus stop. I counted it out, all £7. 12 shillings. Of course this was not the first time I had ever had money of my own, but this was different. It was money I had earned myself. I was at last independent. I was seventeen years old, but tonight I would go down to The Duck's Nest and drink with the best of them. I was under-aged for drinking but who cared. I had spent so much time away from Castletown they probably didn't even know how old I was!

The hours were long at Davis Charlton. I would have to start by 7.45 in the morning and often work through until 7 o'clock at night. Most of the time I would be expected to work Saturday mornings, and often Sundays as well. The overtime was compulsory and just about anything was a sackable offence. A very high percentage of the staff were sacked, and some of the folks I was working with had been sacked several times in the past and more or less treated regular sacking as part of company policy. Mr Hefin Davis had the most notorious temper and would frequently turn up on the shop floor, shouting and bawling, slinging hammers and spanners around and sometimes sacking staff as he wandered through the factory. I can't in all honesty say it was a pleasure working at Davis Charlton, but at least I went home every night and was earning a wage whilst I was still learning. It was certainly an education and prepared me well for the coming years. I remember Taffy, as Hefin Davies was affectionately known by the workforce, taking me aside one day and giving me advice that has stood me in good stead right up until today. "Tom," he said, "in here you are surrounded by people who will cut themselves from time to time. That's what happens in factories, the difference is, they will simply go to the first aid box, stick a plaster on their finger and write down the accident in the book. In your case, every time you cut yourself it will be put down to your being blind and maybe carrying out unsuitable work. You will not simply be allowed to have ordinary accidents in the same way that your colleagues have. Also you will always have to be very good, if not the best at whatever you do, for any shortcomings in your work will also be put down to your disability. Other folks around you will always be indifferent in their work, but it will always be acceptable for them to have different standards. They will simply be good at what they do or not so good. In your case, if you make mistakes, it will nearly always be attributed to your blindness." I didn't take his advice too seriously at the time but I have certainly learnt since that there was much truth in what he said. Still, at least this was the boss who was saying these things, and if he had worked this out for himself then surely I didn't have too much to worry about.

I got on really well with the rest of the workforce. Obviously, at first, they found the situation a little difficult, most of them had never had much, if anything, to do with a blind person, let alone work with one. I struck up an especially good relationship with Stanley. He was another Welshman, but for some reason which I never quite figured out, he was never referred to as Taffy. He worked just down the line from me and at every tea-break or lunch hour he would turn up at my machine like clockwork to guide me down through the machines to the staff room. If he was going in to Douglas at lunch time then I would go with him. His jokes and humour often brought light relief to the shop floor when Taffy was in one of his dangerous moods and was marauding his way along the shop floor shouting and bawling and occasionally sacking.

For some reason, one of the departments of Government had asked that a Royal National Institute for the Blind employment officer be brought over from London. I think it was to check up on the work I was doing and basically to make sure everything was as it should be, whatever that was meant to be. He came and spent a day or two with me and must have told Taffy that I should be using a white stick in order to get around the place. I still had my hang-ups about white sticks and didn't feel the need for one. There were plenty of workers coming in on the same bus as me and getting around the factory wasn't a problem with folks such as Stanley around. Unfortunately, Taffy took the R.N.I.B. man's advice literally and the next morning he announced that anyone seen helping me around the factory or to the bus stop from the factory would be sacked. The effect of this was quite devastating. It made the workforce frightened to come near me and I now had to adapt from only using the stick when absolutely necessary to using it for just about every move even one of just a few yards. In the factory, this was not too bad, but getting from the factory to the bus stop up on the main road was now a bit of a problem. The factory was down in Hills Meadow. Just across the way from the factory was a container depot where large wagons were coming and going all the time. There were no pavements down in the meadow so it was extremely difficult to navigate with a white stick, as there was nothing to follow. There were no walls, no pavements, and every night at five o'clock, I went into battle with the wagons and other vehicles in the meadow. There was only one thing for it. A guide dog. I would apply for a guide dog. That would solve the problem. There was only one snag and that was selling the idea to Taffy. Surely this eccentric Welshman would not tolerate a guide dog on his premises. None of the workforce thought so, and neither did I, but we were all wrong. I asked him could I apply and he agreed; not only did he agree, but he also promised to pay me half my wages while I was across the water in Bolton for a month, training with the dog.

In 1975 I was one of the youngest people, at twenty-two, to qualify for a guide dog. In order to do so it was necessary to stay near the training centre at Bolton for a period of one month. My dog, a golden Labrador named York, was introduced to me on the second day. Each day I would walk the streets of Bolton with York and my instructor, who had also trained York. His name was Bob Steele and we became great friends. At first, the dog showed little interest in his new owner, as the trainer was the only human of any consequence in his life. A dog's affections have slowly to be transferred from its trainer to its new owner. This is called the bonding process and it can take a couple of weeks. On rare occasions the bonding just doesn't take place, and in this event the proposed guide-dog owner would have to try again with a different dog. Every day, Bob would walk a little bit further away from York and me, as we tried to bond and become accustomed to each other. Eventually Bob would be walking behind us and out of sight of York. When this was achieved, the bonding had taken place and the dog was finally working for and indeed trusting his new owner. Whilst I was at the Bolton training centre I was taught such things as how to feed the dog correctly, as it is important not to over feed a guide dog. Overweight dogs lack fitness and are prone to various medical problems, not dissimilar to humans, in fact. I also learned how to groom a dog. This, too, is a very important part of looking after a dog as it helps to locate any problems in the dog's coat, such as mites, and removing the surplus fur makes the dog generally feel better. There were also the dog obedience classes and teaching the dog good social skills. The month at Bolton soon passed and I emerged as a qualified guide-dog owner, free to bring York back to spend the rest of his days on the Isle of Man. Our instructor, Bob, was to accompany us back to the Island to spend a couple of weeks with us, overseeing any problems and helping both myself and York to adjust to our new partnership.

We sailed back to the Island on the *Ben-my-Chree* and it was fitting that her captain was my old friend, Captain Jack Ronan. Of course, he looked after us in the way that by now I had come to expect from Captain Jack. When we stepped out on to the quay at Douglas, a reporter from the *Isle of Man Examiner* was there to meet us and of course the next day there was the expected headline "Wonder Dog Comes to the Island." Bob, who had looked after me so well in Bolton, now set about teaching York the streets of Douglas

(Above) The author, left, at the Bolton Training Centre where he became one of the youngest ever to qualify as a guide-dog owner.

(Right) This picture, from the front page of the 'Isle of Man Examiner' in April 1975, shows the author arriving on Douglas pier with York, the golden Labrador which became his constant companion for many years.

and Castletown. He also had to sort out arrangements at the factory, as York would be coming to work with me every day. Bob was a good negotiator and he would need those skills in abundance when dealing with Taffy.

There was no chance of Taffy allowing the dog to spend his time in the factory in a dog bed. No, York would have to stay outside in a kennel. The kennel wasn't even allowed to be placed on the grass lawn in front of the office windows. Taffy insisted that it had to be erected down on the concrete car park in front of the main building. This would have been alright under certain circumstances, but at Davis Charlton, where I often had to work an eleven-hour day, the days were often long and boring for poor old York. In the wintertime it was particularly unpleasant for him, as it would be cold and the cold south-easterlies would blow relentlessly into his kennel. It certainly wouldn't happen to-day, but in 1974 the industrialist businessmen certainly wielded the power and what they said usually went. Although the Guide Dog Association had its standards, which I am sure it more or less lived up to, I guess it was necessary to compromise with the likes of Taffy, or folks such as me simply would not ever have had guide dogs. If the same situation were to prevail today, I would simply give up one or the other, that is, the dog or the job. But jobs were few and far between and I knew how difficult it would be to find another, so I had to be somewhat grateful for what I had. I hated keeping York in those conditions and dreaded the winter months.

Chapter Twenty-two

As far as my independence was concerned, it was now better than ever; I could go when and wherever I wanted. My mad week-ends in Douglas came to a halt and I stayed local in the Castletown area where I could walk from place to place with York. Taffy's insistence that I went everywhere with a stick, was, I suppose, Taffy's own way of teaching me independence, but I must admit that I didn't see it that way at the time. When I look back, however, it had all the hallmarks of the advice he had earlier given me about the cuts and being the best at whatever work I was doing.

Despite York's difficulties at work, we did go on to have lots of wonderful adventures together. He was inclined to be a bit of a thief and like most Labradors he would eat, if you allowed him, until he died. I once came out of the Chinese take-away in Castletown with York and proceeded to walk the half a mile or so to my home. As I was crossing the busy Castletown by-pass, I dropped my curried king prawns all over the road. Even though these prawns were piping hot, York would not move on until he had licked up every single one. The waiting cars and vans pipped their horns and shouted to me from their wound-down windows that it was all clear for me to cross the remainder of the road. But York would have none of it. We did not move one single step until he had finished snorting his way through the hot, mouth-burning takeaway.

Several years later, when York was about nine or ten years old, I decided to accompany my friend, David Handscombe, who was returning from Navy leave, back to Liverpool, on a day-return trip on the ferry. My brother, Kevin, and, of course, York, came with us. We were sitting in the passenger saloon, with York sleeping on the floor, when two passengers who had been seated opposite us sauntered off to the buffet bar. They returned with two pies, which they placed on the knee-high table that separated us, and then went back to the buffet bar to fetch their cups of tea. Whilst they were gone, York rose to his feet and in two bites swallowed the two pies. On their return the two passengers promptly accused my friend, David, of swiping their pies. He protested his innocence and explained that the dog had nicked them. This didn't wash with our fellow passengers at all as they retorted, "He is a guide dog, and we know that they do not do things like that." Despite the fact that both my brother and I were witnesses to York's theft, we decided it would be much more fun to allow David to take the blame, and of course we didn't want to tarnish the public's "butter wouldn't melt in the mouth" image of guide dogs.

At the factory I tried to make York's time there as comfortable as possible. I acquired a bus seat from the bus company for his kennel, and at lunch times I always tried to obtain a bone from a butcher in Douglas in a bid to prevent the dog from becoming too bored during the long hours spent outside in the kennel. The kennel did have a wire cage attached to it so at least he could go outside; but he could only walk a few paces, and the whole set-up was really far from satisfactory. I was in no position to argue with Taffy. It wasn't a question of which did I want most, the guide dog or the job. I needed both and the only way I could have both was to conform to Taffy's weird human- and dog-management ways. In the end it was York himself who solved the problem, if indeed solved is the right word. It took York six years to resolve our situation but eventually he did indeed take the matter into his own hands - or should I say paws.

In my eight years working for Taffy I had seen many staff come and go, indeed it was unusual to go for a full week without a riot of some sort taking place on the shop floor. The parting of the ways between Taffy and myself was brought about by the re-seeding of the grass lawn outside the office windows. Taffy blew into the factory that morning and announced that the lawn had been re-seeded and while the seed was growing, no one was to set foot in this area. Of course, he concluded this statement with his usual line: "Anyone setting foot in this area will be sacked." The trouble was, York did not hear this from Taffy and that lunchtime, as soon as I released him from his kennel, he made straight for the forbidden ground. With York's paw marks deeply scored in the soil, the evidence was rather stacked against us, and although my workmates put up a spirited defence by insisting that the canine paw marks could have come from any dog in the area, I was sacked on the spot. I think York was delighted when I turned up with his lead and harness to go home at two o'clock in the afternoon. It was not unusual to be sacked by Taffy and I wasn't unduly concerned about my dismissal. After all, on one occasion he had sacked the entire workforce, over a hundred men and women. Everyone was reinstated the next day. It seems that he had had some kind of row with a Government department and threatened them with firing all his staff. He carried out his threat, then made a phone call to the Government department confirming that he had done so. Once they backed down he promptly reinstated everyone.

I walked the half mile or so down to The Quarterbridge pub, where I knew I could have a pint and then catch the next bus to Castletown. The locals and staff of The Quarterbridge didn't seem too surprised about my predicament. It was a pub Davis Charlton workers often frequented, and sacked workers were ten a penny as far as they were concerned. After a pint or two I boarded the bus for Castletown. By the time I reached home, some thirty minutes later, a reporter from the *Isle of Man Examiner* was already waiting for me. Well, why not? I suppose they had a great story. "Blind man sacked because guide dog trespasses on forbidden lawn." Of course, the phone rang the next day offering me my job back. It was way too late, the headline was already winging its way around the Island. To Taffy's eternal credit, he did not respond to the newspaper article with the all too familiar, "No comment." He fought back predictably like the Taffy we all knew. But his position was hopeless. The kind of brawls he was used to having were fine when confined to the shop floor, but out in the public eye and under scrutiny from all and sundry, he didn't have a chance. Mind you, neither did I. It was, and only ever could be, a battle neither of us could win. Members of the House of Keys came and went. More stories appeared in the newspapers. It was the talk of the Island in 1978.

The Union got involved, even though I wasn't a member. Taffy forbade membership of a trade union. Eventually it was decided that a tribunal would be set up to deal with the matter. When I inquired as to what was the best I could expect from this tribunal, I was informed that they might rule that Taffy would have to give me my job back. I instructed them to drop the tribunal, as there seemed little point in going on with it. I couldn't possibly go back to Taffy after all this publicity; it simply couldn't work now. Of course, Taffy did not remain on my Christmas card list. Well, not for a year or two. Taffy was a slightly mad, eccentric Welshman. I don't believe he was a vindictive man, he simply treated me exactly the way he treated everybody else. Had it not been a high profile case, brought about by the press coverage of what had happened, I probably would have simply gone back to work for Taffy just like many others had done before me. He wasn't a bad man, in fact he probably did more for me than many others. He gave me a job at a time when perhaps no one else would have done. He treated me exactly the same as the rest of his workforce, which is something blind people are always telling everyone is what they want. I learned a great deal in the eight years I was at Davies Charlton. Indeed, when I think back to those days, I have more fond memories of Taffy than bad ones. I'm sure that if we had been introduced to each other under different circumstances, we may well have become life-long friends.

Chapter Twenty-three

I soon got used to life without Davies Charlton. There was no hanging around wondering what to do with myself. York knew what he was doing when he took his lunchtime break on Taffy's lawn. It was after one of those long walks that we both now had time for, that I met up with Bill Swain, a local businessman, in that favourite old pub of mine, The Duck's Nest. Bill ran a small factory just outside the village of Ballasalla. On hearing of my plight, he immediately offered me some part-time employment, packing components and doing some inspection work. It wasn't exactly engineering, but it was cash in hand and, because it involved only working for about four hours a day, in the afternoon, it left the morning free for York and I to roam freely over the beach and Langness. The kennel was transferred from Davis Charlton to Bill's factory, but this time placed on the grass just outside the factory. York could now come into the factory to join us when the weather was inclement. I had the best of both worlds. There was plenty of time for walking and fishing with Michael. York loved coming out in the boat, especially when the trip was over and we were nearing the harbour. As we entered the harbour mouth, he would leap over the side and swim all the way to the shore, sometimes a distance of several hundred yards. Once his paws touched the beach, he would run round and round in circles, totally engulfed in the pride of his achievement. Poor old York, he had not had much of a life before, but he was sure making up for it now. Bill's factory was about two miles from my house, so it was within easy walking distance for York and me. York had now completely transformed our lives. He had taken me from a ten-hour, sometimes seven-day-a-week job, and even worse for himself, to a lifestyle of fishing, swimming and walking. By the time we arrived at Bill's factory, all he wanted to do was lie down and sleep.

I didn't exactly go out looking for full-time work while this situation lasted. I was quite happy working part-time for Bill and the present life-style suited York and me down to the ground. Eventually, full-time work came looking for me by way of Croft Seafoods fish factory. The timing for this change was just about perfect as Bill's factory was already preparing to move to Douglas, and York was now getting old. The little *Siesta* was by now showing signs of age, too, and one unsuspecting day she was towed from her mooring at Derbyhaven and laid to rest on the bottom of Derbyhaven Bay, where she lies until this day. Her replacement was an 18-foot, fibreglass vessel with a powerful inboard engine. She was much faster than the *Siesta,* speed now being of the essence in a more competitive and fast-changing lobster-fishing industry. Michael named her the *Catherine Ann,* after his deceased baby daughter, to whom I have already referred. The Catherine Ann had an open wheel-house. That is to say, we had a box-like structure at the front end of her that had no doors. This was the height of luxury compared to the little *Siesta* as it afforded some protection from breaking waves and a modicum of shelter when the weather was hostile.

My job in the fish factory came about in much the same way as working for Bill Swain did. Terry Croft, a local businessman who had spent many years working in the fish processing industry, decided it would be a good idea for me to go and work for him in his factory in Port St Mary. This proved to be another beneficial change for me, even though the health and hygiene laws meant that York could not come to the fish factory with me. If working there wasn't exactly going to sea for a living, it was as close as I was likely to get. I no longer had any need for my micrometers and so forth. Now the only tools I needed were rubber gloves, smocks and wellies. Croft Seafoods was a shellfish-processing factory, handling mainly scallops and a smaller species known in the Isle of Man as queenies. When the shellfish first came in from the boats, they would be shelled and have all the waste matter removed by a team of women, who were paid on a piecework basis at so much for every pound of fish meat they produced. The fish would then proceed to me and a gang of others, and we would clean them, which we did by means of placing them in a wire basket and shaking them under a hose pipe. Then we would take the queenies or scallops and place them on steel trays. Once all the trays were full, they would be loaded on to trolleys and wheeled into a blast freezer. On completion of this procedure, the trolleys would be pulled out from the freezer, and the queenies and scallops removed from the trays, placed into bags and boxed. The boxes of processed fish would then be put into storage freezers to await shipment to Europe or wherever the best price could be obtained.

In the summertime, the hours could be long, sometimes from seven in the morning until midnight. If the weather was good and lots of boats had been out, we would have to remain at the factory until all the landed fish had been either processed or at least placed in cold storage. In the winter it was very often the complete opposite. If the weather was bad and the boats had not been to sea, there would be little to do in the factory. This was not good news for the girls, who were only paid for the work they produced. In my case, I, like the rest of the permanent staff, was on a flat rate of pay. This meant that in the summertime, when the place was busy and the hours were long, I just got the basic pay. However, at times in winter when there was little work, I still received the same rate of pay. In summertime, and especially at weekends, when I would want to get finished so that I could get to the pub, my brother Kevin would come in and help me clear the backlog. However, during the winter when the days are long, there was only so much cleaning and maintenance that we could do.

It was on one of these winter days that my boss announced that he and a few others were going off to the pub for the rest of the afternoon. I usually went with them when this happened, but for reasons for which I cannot recall, on this occasion I was to stay behind at the factory. I probably was not best pleased about this and as he was about to leave I asked: "So, what about me, then. What do you want me to do for the rest of the afternoon?" "As far as I'm concerned, you can paint the factory," he said. I sat in the canteen pondering the situation. No, I was not going to sit here all afternoon and if he wants his factory painting then that's what he can have. I knew where the paint was kept and within a few minutes I had set about my task. I painted everything, cupboards, doors and walls. I kept going until I ran out of paint. If I had had more, I might have gone on to paint the whole of Port St Mary. By the time he came back, I had gone home. When I returned to the factory the next day the atmosphere was certainly tense, but of course they couldn't exactly sack me, they would have looked pretty stupid sacking a blind man for painting their factory when he had only been carrying out instructions. Of course, once the mess had been cleared up and enough time had lapsed, everybody saw the funny side of it. I don't remember ever being left behind again on quiet days when management was going to the pub.

Something special seemed to happen every week-end, and there was always something unique to talk about in the factory every Monday morning. On Saturday afternoons we would usually go for a trip out to another town or for a few pints in a pub somewhere off the beaten track. It was always nice to have few drinks with folks I hadn't seen for a long time. One particular Saturday, my friend Bobby and I set off to have a drink or two in The Baltic Inn, a small pub about five miles north of Castletown in the village of Foxdale. Bobby was something of a character and had one glass eye. That meant we had three glass eyes or one real eye between the two of us. He drove a little Robin Reliant three-wheel motor car, and it was in this little gem that we went off to Foxdale. We had only just started on our way back to Castletown when a police car stopped us. I don't know why the police thought we looked a bit dodgy but they were obviously quite right in their assessment. As the constable approached the driver's side of the car, Bobby decided to get out and remonstrate with him. This he did in the middle of the road, leaving the engine running and the driver's door wide open into the road. With Bobby and the constable standing in the middle of the road, finding it difficult to agree on anything and holding up the traffic behind us, I heard Bobby say to him, "Now, excuse me, constable, but me and my friend, Mr Glassey here, are on our way back to Castletown, and we only have one eye between us. Now don't you think we have enough problems without you adding to them?" I think the constable gave us about fifteen minutes to get our car off the road which was about ten minutes more than we needed.

Chapter Twenty-four

I f Bobby was a character then so was my brother, Kevin who was happy-go-lucky, a laugh a minute, and life to him was just a barrel of fun. Bobby was more the likeable rogue type of person. When you were out with Kevin you just never knew quite what was going to happen next. He had a special presence. He could walk into any sleepy country pub on a Saturday afternoon and within ten minutes of his arrival folks who had been quietly sitting there chatting to each other would be laughing themselves silly. He made weekends special for whoever he came into contact with.

Friday, October 10th, 1979, was no different from any other normal Friday. I was expecting Kevin to turn up at the factory at his usual time; but at some point during the afternoon my boss decided he was coming through to Castletown for a change and therefore would give me a lift. I phoned Kev and told him he had no need to make the trip to Port St Mary as I would be coming through to Castletown with my boss, and I would meet up with him in the pub later. We finished our work, and the boss and I set off for Castletown and commenced our night out. Kev did not appear and I assumed that he had met up with some mates and become involved in a session elsewhere. The night passed and I went home whilst the boss headed off in a taxi back to Port St Mary. I was in bed fast asleep when it happened. There is something very distinctive about a policeman's knock. It is heavy and rings throughout the house as though it means business, especially in the early hours of the morning. It can never be confused with the knock of a neighbour who although trying to rouse

134

you is also timid of waking you. The policeman's knock is purpose-
ful and is designed to drag you from your sleep to pay attention.

During my silent moments I can still hear my mother's cries as she
stood at the bottom of the stairs. I did not hear what the policeman
was saying. I didn't need to. At the age of twenty-three, Kevin was
dead. I made my way down the stairs and by now Sergeant Jones was
in the living room and Mother was sobbing by the fireplace. I don't
recall Sergeant Jones actually telling me that Kevin was dead. He
may have done, I wasn't listening and I didn't need to. Maybe I did-
n't actually want to have it spelled out to me. For just those few
moments if I hadn't heard it spelled out to me, then there was just a
chance that it might not have happened. When something like this
happens you tend to cling to the few precious intervening seconds
that lapse between what you want to believe and the awful truth being
borne in upon you. This was unimaginable. This was worse than anything that had ever happened before. It made those dark going-back-
to-school days seem like picnics. I left the room and climbed the
stairs. I walked into my parents' bedroom. Dad was still sleeping. I
stood for a second or two feeling like the executioner. I was about to
bring him from his peaceful sleep and deal him an unhealable blow.
I remember pulling him by the arm and then, when he did wake, I bot-
tled out. I couldn't tell him. I told him to come downstairs, that something terrible had happened, and left the room so that he could not ask
any follow-up questions. I just could not bring myself to part with the
words: "Kevin is dead".

Although Kev was not a sailor and had never spent much time at
sea, he loved the water. He worked with Dad unloading boats in
Castletown and Port St Mary. Often before coming home after a night
out, he would wander down to the harbour for an hour or so and just
sit there fascinated by the movement of the tide and the general activity of the harbour. He was not a swimmer, but that didn't deter him or
induce any fear of water. However, it was not the sea that had claimed
him, but a swimming bath. You might think midnight was a strange
time to go swimming: but it was customary for some of the locals,
after a few drinks on a Friday night, to take a dip in the baths belonging to King William's College. Kevin had gone there with his mates
as on many other occasions in the past. Even though he did not swim,
he still enjoyed a dip in the pool. We never really found out exactly

what happened. His friends who had been with him on that night explained how they had been for a dip and everything was normal. When they left the pool Kevin stayed back saying he would be along shortly. He always did want that extra five minutes, whether it applied to a lie-in in the morning or at chucking-out time in the pub. It would have been perfectly normal for him to re-act in that way. When the lads returned to the poolside later to hurry him along, they found him floating in the water.

No one blamed them in any way for what happened; it really was just one of those unfortunate accidents. Sometimes things happen when it is simply nobody's fault, but sometimes we are unable to accept something until someone has been made responsible for what has happened. I blamed the College for their lack of security in leaving the baths unlocked. I blamed myself, for if I had not changed arrangements at the fish factory and let him come and pick me up as normal, it wouldn't have happened. You can go on blaming yourself and others for the rest of your life. At the end of the day, if accidents didn't happen and if Fate didn't play its hand, we would all live to be old men and women, and coroners would be unemployed, and there would be no need for inquests.

It was a long night, the night of October 10th, 1979. I remember leaving Mother, Father, Sergeant Jones and other family members who had gathered at the house by now, and returning to my bedroom. I lay on my bed and couldn't stand the quiet, so I turned on the radio. Whatever station the radio was tuned into had closed down, and the only sound that could be heard was the hiss of the ether. I refrained from turning the radio off. I needed to hear that hiss, as without it it seemed that the world had ended. That background hiss sort of signified that the world had not ended. The next morning, on Manx Radio, Kevin was the lead story on the news. It sounded so cold and matter of fact, I felt like smashing the radio. Did the newsreader not know he was talking about my brother; he wasn't just Kevin Glassey, a landscape gardener. This wasn't just anyone. Of course it was and today, whenever I hear some tragic accident being reported on the radio, I do not just hear the words on the airwaves, I can feel the pain that those concerned are going through.

I suppose one funeral is much like any other. They are devastating for the family, friends and loved ones, and a pain in the neck for those who attend simply because they feel they must, or feel that they are obliged to in some way. The priest went through the usual thing that priests do. "The Lord giveth and the Lord taketh." After the service was over, most folks found their way to Kevin's local, The Ship, in Castletown. I remember standing at the bar, the pub full of mourners. I didn't want to be there, this was just going through the motions and I'd had enough of that with the funeral service. I sloped away quietly only to be followed by Dad into the hallway. He tried to persuade me to come and have a drink with him, but I was not having it. Ten minutes later I was at home in bed, away from everyone, away from the event. As I lay there in bed, I suddenly felt guilty. I should have stayed with Dad, he would be finding it hard, too. I got up and dressed and returned to the scene and continued with the process of going through the motions. The following day it was all over, of course, but it would never be all over. Life could not and would not ever be the same again. It is said that time is a great healer; I don't think that time heals anything. I think that as time goes by you think of these things less often. At any given time, the pain can return and when it does it can be just as sharp as it ever was. It simply doesn't last as long and the intervals grow longer.

There was now myself, plus Lenny, my older brother, Sean, my younger brother, and Mum and Dad, all living at King William's Way, Janet's Corner, Castletown. Slowly, very slowly, some kind of normality returned. Everyone mucked in and I think we all lived one day at a time. I don't think any of us ever become battle-tough to the extent that we become immune to whatever Fate deals us. Mother and Father had already been through my problems as a child, and Auntie Mary's and Granny's accident outside their front door in Ballasalla, and now this. I don't think it matters how many blows you are dealt, they cut into you just as deeply and never heal completely.

Kevin had spent most of his twenty-three years on this planet laughing. He landed on the funny side of everything, and even at such times as when he found himself in something of a precarious situation, it usually ended in laughter. His fascination with the sea, boats or anything to do with water, meant that he simply could not pass the harbour without gazing for long periods at moored boats, a duck or simply something just floating on the water. On his way home one night after a few drinks in a local pub, he decided to board a rowing boat that was moored at the quayside just outside the pub. In order to board the vessel it was necessary to shin his way down the mooring line. After remaining on board the boat for some time he realised that getting back on shore again was going to be something of a problem. With no ladder handy the only method of coming ashore was to climb up the mooring line he had earlier shinned down. With several pints consumed and late at night, which meant it was also dark, he started his ascent from the small boat. After climbing a short distance his arms became tired and were unable to support his weight. Soon his legs were trailing in the water and he was clinging to the rope for dear life. He started shouting at the top of his voice for help. Eventually a passer-by advised him to let go of the rope. Not being able to swim he was very reluctant to do so. To his absolute horror his new-found friend on the quayside then untied the rope. His legs, which were flailing about in the water, now sank the remaining eighteen inches to the bottom and he simply walked ashore! He had not realised that the tide was almost out and that there had only been about two feet of water in the harbour. He could easily have waded to the jetty at any time!

Chapter Twenty-five

I did not return to the fish factory after Kevin's death. The fish factory by then was only ticking over and was shedding some of its permanent staff, so it seemed that this was as good a time as any to bring this particular venture to an end. For some time I had no regular work, so in order to keep me occupied and to put a few bob in my pocket, Dad set me up with around two hundred chickens. This grew to about three hundred at its peak. Dad also had a large greenhouse that could house up to nine or ten dozen tomato plants. So between the tomatoes and the chickens, and a bit of financial assistance from Uncle Sean, who had by now moved from London and bought himself a pub in County Tipperary in Ireland, I got by pretty well.

The chickens and the greenhouse were on a small parcel of land that Dad had started to rent just before he left the Gas Works. He had since bought the land for a small fee as a sitting tenant. It was only about half an acre and was directly under the flight path into Ronaldsway Airport, which meant it would never be used for any development. In the past we had kept pigs, cattle, sheep and goats there. Dad had taught me how to milk the goats and when he was tied up on wrong shifts at the Gas Works, or emptying coal boats, and couldn't get home in time, I would do the milking. On many occasions the goats would kick over the bucket just as I was finishing and I would arrive home without enough milk to soak the cornflakes. I always loved being with the animals and with the goats especially. This was reciprocated, as they would always kick up a horrendous din when it was time for me to leave them. They always managed to give me a guilt complex as I would hear them bleating all the way along the road home, which was about a quarter of a mile or so. It was almost like dropping off young (human) kids at school.

So now, with my chickens to let out and feed, and tomatoes to water, I had good cause to be up at five in the mornings, which suited me well as I have always loved early mornings. In the summer I would often lie in bed waiting for the song thrush to lead the birds into the dawn chorus. As soon as the concert was underway, I would be up and gone. York was not quite so active as he had been, but he could still manage a four-mile walk. I didn't take him out with me in the boat any more as he was now becoming arthritic. Still, we would wander out to Derbyhaven and sit on the breakwater for half an hour, with a flask. Then we would wander back to Castletown along the promenade, a walk of about a mile or so, ironically calling in at King William's College on the way.

I had become great friends with the ground staff there by now and they were more than happy to allow York to roam freely on their well-manicured rugby and cricket pitches. I would always stop off and have a mug of tea with them in their shack before carrying on home. Jackie Bond, the former captain of Lancashire County Cricket Club, was the head groundsman, and although I had no interest in cricket, I loved to sit and listen to his stories of some of the great players he had played with and the places he had visited. His assistant was a man called Len Oddie. Len was a lovely person who possessed a fantastic knowledge of wildlife. Sometimes he would come and collect me from home in the evening and we would go and sit on the banks of the Silverburn at Rushen Abbey where he would teach me the various bird songs. It made such a difference once I had learnt to identify their calls, as now I could sit in the park or in a field and be able to recognise the different species, rather than just be able to hear a chorus of birdsong and not know which was which.

Once the tea and the chat were over at King Bill's, I would continue on my way to let out and feed the hens and so on. On one of these mornings I had set off early for Derbyhaven with York. On arrival, I released York to go and do his own thing on the beach, as was normal. As I sat on a rock quietly having a smoke, I heard York scratching and digging in the sand. After a short while, I decided to go and assist him. He was pawing the sand frantically and so I bent down and scratched away with him. Eventually, I discovered a length of rope so I pulled at the rope and York dug like hell in the sand. Soon we both unearthed an object. I was by now wildly excited. It was made of metal or iron and although it was covered in sand I could clearly feel that letters were engraved on it. I hoisted it up and over my shoulder, believing I had found some real treasure and would probably make enough money from the sale of it to keep me in beer money, and York in dog food, for life. I hauled this treasure trove all the way back to King Bill's on my back, where I knew Len would be able to identify it. I arrived at Len's shack exhausted and pretty damned excited only to hear Len say: "What the hell are you doing hauling a bloody fire grate around with you?" Someone had obviously slung it out on to the beach, but I bet they didn't guess it would end up in King William's College bin!

Life rolled along pretty much in this vein for some time. I lived for the early mornings; I just loved being up with the larks. In summer I had a big advantage over everyone else in as much as I only had to tell myself it was a beautiful day, and it would be. There was many a time I would return to the house and comment on what a fantastic day it was, only for someone to say, no, it's cloudy, or misty, or whatever. The truth was, and still is, it is they who were missing out. One of the advantages of being totally blind is that so long as it's not raining then every day can be as beautiful as you want it to be. No day is ever spoiled by waking up and looking out of the window, believing what your eyes tell you, and returning to bed. The weather only plays a minor part in what constitutes a beautiful day.

As time passed by and York grew older, eventually not moving from his bed in the living room, inevitably the time came for him to say "bye, bye" and bow out. He had not got off to a great start for a guide dog, stuck in that lousy kennel at Davis Charlton. He had sure made up for it since. He had spent the second half of his life roaming the beaches, swimming in Derbyhaven Bay and tramping up and down the Silverburn River. The only work he did for the second half of his life was guiding me from one adorable place to the next.

I was not making very much money from the chickens, and with the stock ageing, and roaming dogs having killed off about a quarter of the flock, it was time to move on to something else. Once more, it was Dad who came to the rescue. He was still landscaping, which was fine for the summer, but in winter the harsh Island weather could mean that you could go for long periods without being able to work. A large shed was duly built, a contract with the Forestry Board signed, and we were in the log business. The logs, or tree trunks to be precise, were purchased from the Forestry Board and then split and bagged for firewood. My job was on the log-splitter. The log-splitter was a large, steel contraption that sat on a wooden bench. It had a large axe shaped blade welded to one end of it, and an hydraulic ram at the other. The timber was placed on the steel frame up against the axe-like blade; then, by turning the lever to the left, the ram was sent forwards, pushing the timber against the steel blade, which in turn would pass through the timber, splitting the log in half. Turning the lever to the right brought the ram back to its fixed position, the split logs then being free to fall into the sack that was attached to the splitter. The splitter was powered by an old International tractor, which probably would have graced any museum. However, it hardly ever let us down. The log business provided us with a steady income for many a winter. We weren't exactly making megga bucks, but it did keep me out of trouble and kept me occupied. There were three of us: my brother Lenny, who drove the wagon and went out with the deliveries; me on the splitter, and Dad who did just about everything.

One evening, I came home from a hard day's splitting and decided to go for a tea-time pint as was my wont. Mother gave me a lift to The Duck's Nest, which was the norm with York no longer with us. I told her I would ring her later in order that she could come and collect me to take me home. While I was in the pub, my old mate Michael turned up. He had gone back to the Steam Packet for the summer and was sailing to Fleetwood in about an hour, returning light-ship the same night. Of course, within a twinkling, I had left the pub and was soon on board the *Ben-my-Chree* bound for Fleetwood. On our arrival in Fleetwood we were to discharge our passengers and sail back to Douglas empty. Once there, I had just enough time to nip ashore to phone mother. "Okay, you have stayed a bit late," she said. "Are you ready to come home now?" "Yes, Mother," I replied, "but I don't think you will make it in the car. I'm in Fleetwood." I don't think she had ever heard of Fleetwood, but nonetheless I think she got the picture. Of course, I sailed home with the ship and by midnight I was

142

(Above) The author with one of his best mates, Michael Quine, passing Ailsa Craig during a trip to Ardrossan.

(Right) The author with his now-elderly York in the garden at King William's Way, Janet's Corner, Castletown.

tucked up in my own bed having travelled about 150 miles since I left for my tea-time pint about seven hours earlier.

A week later I joined Michael once again on the same ship, this time bound for Ardrossan, leaving Douglas at mid-day on Saturday and returning at the same time on the Sunday. Captain Jack was the master of the vessel and it was a real pleasure to sail with him once again after so many years. It was also nice to be sailing with Captain Jack to somewhere I actually wanted to go, as opposed to somewhere I had to go to. We landed in Ardrossan at 6 p.m., and once the passengers and cars had all been off-loaded we trooped ashore for a night on the beer in Ardrossan. When we returned to the ship, somewhat the worse for wear, and not before we had boarded the wrong ship, it became apparent that we had not fixed up my sleeping arrangements. In haste, I was shoved into the forward passenger saloon. This was fine, but what I didn't know was that the stewardesses' sleeping-quarters were just off this lounge. Of course, when I boarded the ship they were all fast asleep, but when they surfaced in the morning they decided they had a stowaway on board. A frantic woman shaking me by the arm awoke me. "What the hell do you think you are doing?" she said. I figured that she might not know Michael, so I said: "I'm with the captain." "Oh, yes, they all say that!" she said. She then told her two colleagues to stay with me whilst she went for the captain. I knew she was going to return all embarrassed so I started practising my "don't worry - it's okay, - anyone can make a mistake, love" routine. I started to blurt it out as she came through the door, only to hear her say: "I couldn't find him so you had better stay put where you are." Fortunately, the chief officer turned up to take me for breakfast and saved my bacon, so to speak. Needless to say, my new friend, the stewardess, took good care of me all the way back to Douglas.

During the winter the logging kept the wolf from the door, so in order to earn a crust or two in the summer I took up making wicker cradles. The problem was that there were plenty of cheap imports from the Far East, so in order to give the product a local twist I needed to have the wooden frames made on the Island. This meant I could have my own designs and also helped to make the products a little special. I needed to find someone with a jigsaw and enough time on their hands to make the frames. I found the answer to this problem, not on the Isle of Man itself, but on the small island, known as the Calf of Man, about half a mile off its southern tip. A good friend of mine, Geordie Adamson, was employed by the Northern Lighthouse Board, and had been stationed at the Calf of Man Lighthouse. Geordie had originally come to the Isle of Man from the Orkney Islands. He was one of those people who could do anything with his hands and we referred to him as Mister Fix-it. Geordie and his wife, Margaret, lived in the lighthouse buildings in Port St Mary. He, along with two other keepers, would spend one month on the Calf and then be relieved by another keeper, in effect working for one month on the Calf followed by a month at home. The Calf of Man was a lonely place to be, with just the three lighthouse keepers and one resident bird warden, making a total population of four. There was not a lot of distraction. In fact, the Calf was the perfect place on which to set up a small, off-shore industry. I would buy the timber from Qualtrough's timberyard in Castletown and send it out to Geordie on the lighthouse tender which left Port St Mary every couple of days with mail and food supplies. Geordie would send the finished frames back to me by the same method. I did make the occasional trip out to the Calf on the tender just to check on my off-shore business venture; and after a glass of rum I would return to the mainland fully satisfied that all was well. This arrangement worked out very well, and I am sure that even today there are a few cradles or plant-pot holders somewhere on the Island that were in part made on the Calf of Man. The Calf of Man Lighthouse is now unmanned, along with all the other lighthouses on the Isle of Man, and Geordie has retired, but we have kept in touch and remain good friends.

Chapter Twenty-six

I had known Barbara for a long time, but until now only as a lady who at week-ends worked as a television rent collector for a local TV rental firm. She called at the house every Saturday morning and would have a cup of tea or something before carrying on with her telly round. Barbara had moved over to the Island from St Helens in 1972, and lived in the village of St John's. She loved animals and, in particular, dogs, and I guess it was dogs that brought us together. By now I had another guide dog, a Labrador called Waldo. I used to ask Barbara quite often what she did on Sundays. "Catching up with housework, et cetera," was her reply. On one particular Saturday she asked me why I wanted to know. So I suggested she might like to go for a walk with her dog and mine. She agreed to call the next day at 1 p.m. and we took the dogs for a run. On this occasion we decided to climb South Barrule, a mountain in the south of the Island which has a peak of about 1,500 feet. I guess this was a pretty good start, as if you climb a mountain with someone on your first date you must mean business. We had a lot in common; she loves music, is a fine singer and plays the cornet; and we were both into walking so we went on long rambles with the dogs.

After five months going out together, Barbara and I were married in Patrick Church on April 3rd, 1991. Barbara's mother, Jean, her stepfather, Joe, and her sister, Janet, came over for the wedding. We only gave people three weeks notice of our getting married and this,

(Facing page) The author with his bride, Barbara, following their marriage at Patrick Church on 3rd April, 1991.

unfortunately, reduced the number of members of Barbara's family who were available to travel over. The wedding got off to rather a dramatic start with Barbara's stepfather collapsing in her cottage about fifteen minutes before the service was due to start, and when I was already at the church. Joe was meant to be giving Barbara away and his collapse caused a great deal of panic, as you can imagine. Luckily, Ann and Terry Couhig, two of Barbara's friends, had called at the cottage to deliver the bridesmaid, who happened to be their granddaughter, Rebecca. "Are you doing anything in the next hour, Terry?" Barbara asked. "Why?" "Could you give me away?" Terry came to the rescue. It meant that we had the somewhat unusual situation in which the groom thought he was going to be left waiting at the church rather than the bride. Five minutes before the ceremony was due to start, Barbara was giving the doctor instructions on how to find the cottage. Her mother did not see her married as she waited for the doctor to arrive. It was sad, really, as Barbara was the oldest and last to be married, and her mother missed it.

It was a fairly low-key wedding as neither of us wanted a big reception. We held the reception with about 50 family and friends in the Ballacallin Hotel in Dalby. Happily, by the time we arrived at the hotel we had heard that Joe had been diagnosed as having a severe vertigo attack. My best man was a guy called Willy Kneale, who has always been, and still is, a great personal friend. He handled the whole thing brilliantly; and his wife, Patricia, who had once owned a bridal shop, was well versed in the do's and don'ts at weddings and was invaluable in helping out in the absence of Barbara's mother. It was Patricia who had given Barbara her wedding dress. Willie made an ideal best man and, because of our long-standing friendship, he had many stories to tell. When all the singing and dancing was over and all the guests had gone home, Barbara and I wandered back to her, now our, little cottage. Later that evening we found ourselves sitting in the forest eating a bag of fish and chips with only the sound of the birds as a background to the quiet, still, evening air of St John's. A perfect day was over and we returned to our cottage a very happy and contented couple.

(Facing page) Happy scene at the wedding reception held at the Ballacallin Hotel. From left to right is the author's mother-in-law, Jean, his Uncle Billy, the bride and the author, his father, Dennis and mother, Nell.

Willie has always had a heart of gold and I recall the times when, just after I was sacked at Davis Charlton, a ten pound note was pushed through my letter box each week. Although he never owned up to this, I knew that it was Willy on his way home from work, because one night he was spotted by a neighbour. I was already somewhat in debt to Willie. Some twenty years earlier I was partly responsible for his work's van suffering extensive damage. Willie was giving me a lift home after one of my tea-time drinks in The Duck's Nest. Whilst he was trying to reverse the van out of a tight spot, he completely forgot that I was blind and asked, "Are we okay on your side Tom?" Thinking he was joking, I replied, "Well, I can't see anything, Will." The next thing we knew was this almighty bump as we reversed into a telegraph pole. The van suffered a large dint to its rear, and several televisions in the back were given a bit of a jolt. Poor Willie had a fair bit of explaining to do the following morning when he arrived at work!

Willie was, and probably still is, a very good darts player, and at one time played for the Island dart team. I often travelled with the team around the U.K. to the various counties. On one occasion they were playing Warwickshire in Birmingham, and I had travelled with the team as the Island's only supporter. I shared a room with Willie. I have always been an early riser so I found myself up and dressed while Willie was still snoring his head off. Of course, I had a bit of a problem in as much as I did not know my way around the hotel. Frustrated with Willie for sleeping at a time when I wanted to go and explore my new surroundings, I turned his electric blanket up to its maximum and set off on a bit of a mystery tour of the hotel. After wandering along several corridors and following the sound of voices, I eventually found myself sitting down in the hotel dining room. The guys I was sitting with were a very friendly bunch of lads and I gathered they were some kind of pop group who had been playing somewhere in the city the night before. They told me they were called Hot Chocolate, which meant absolutely nothing to me. However, when I later told a very hot and sweaty Willie that I had been down and had my breakfast with a group called Hot Chocolate, he took a fair bit of convincing. Later, I learned from the rest of the team that my breakfast friends were quite well known; and they became even more so when their track, 'I Believe in Miracles', was used in the film, 'The

Full Monty'. Being the only supporter it was thought appropriate that I should wear the team blazer and badge. This caused the opposition some confusion when we all stood in the passageway waiting to be called out into the main hall for the match. I was standing holding Willie's arm when I heard one of the Warwickshire players saying to his teammate: "Bloody hell, Joe, we'll beat this Isle of Man team alright, one of them's bloody blind!"

The author with his close friend and best man, Willie Kneale.

151

Chapter Twenty-seven

The cottage Barbara and I lived in, on the banks of the River Neb, on the Patrick road in the village of St John's, was about eight miles from Castletown, so the log-splitting was now history, not only because of the distance, but also because there was no regular bus service between the two places. From now on, I was to become a house-husband. Barbara worked in Ramsey as an Information Technology Manager for a time-share firm, and set off every morning at about eight o'clock. My guide dog, Waldo, and I would set off to walk to Peel to do the shopping. There was a regular bus service between St John's and Peel but we preferred to walk. We would take the Patrick road in and maybe come back along the Poortown road, a total distance of about eight miles, with me carting a rucksack full of shopping on my back on the return journey. Unfortunately, it was not long before it was discovered that Waldo had severe arthritis and would not be able to continue as a working guide dog.

I had only had Waldo for a short time so this was a great shock. He had to be retired and although I could have kept him as a pet, this would not have been practical as we already had Bess, a Border Collie, and I would have to obtain another guide dog. This would have meant having three dogs in our tiny cottage. What made the situation worse was that Bess, our pet collie, worshipped the ground Waldo walked on. It was a heart-breaking decision to have to hand Waldo back to the training centre, but if I was to have another guide dog, it had to be done. It would have been difficult to manage with-

Escort, the golden retriever, which is the author's third guide-dog and still going strong.

out one living in such an isolated area. Had I still lived in Castletown, I would simply have kept Waldo as a pet since it would have been easier to manage with shops, pubs and everything being so much closer at hand. In due course, Waldo returned to the training centre in Bolton and was eventually re-homed on a farm in Warwickshire. A couple of weeks later I found myself back at the training centre. I came home with a golden retriever called Escort who has continued pretty much where Waldo left off although I can't say that Bess took to him as she did to Waldo.

It would be something of an exaggeration to say that St John's was my Birmingham on the Isle of Man. However, for all its beautiful rolling hills and countryside, it was still three miles from the sea. I don't think I can quite fully take to any place if I can't hear the murmur of the sea when I lay my head down at night. I loved the lack of traffic on the Patrick and Poortown roads as I made my way to and from Peel. I guess there is no better walking area in the whole of the Isle of Man. And living on the banks of the Neb, with the ducks coming up from the river to visit me every day, made it an idyllic setting.

However, our tiny, one-bedroomed cottage was simply too small for the four of us, Barbara, Bess, Escort and myself. With Barbara driving the 17 miles or so to and from Ramsey every day, the answer was obvious - we would move to Ramsey. We sold the cottage to our next-door neighbours, making it possible for them to turn two tiny cottages into one reasonably-sized one. Barbara was now earning a reasonable salary and this enabled us to take out a mortgage on a two-bedroomed bungalow in Claughbane, just above the golf course in Ramsey. It had a large rear garden and within a few steps from the front door we once again were in beautiful forests, this time of the north. As far as the dogs were concerned, Ramsey was paradise. Its wide, sandy beach, the low grasslands of Poyll Dhooie, and the Claughbane woods meant there was any amount of rambling and free running for them within a very short distance of the bungalow.

Ramsey is only eight miles from the very northern tip of the Island, the Point of Ayre. We spent many a week-end camping in the coastal area to its south, known as the Ayres. There were, of course, no facilities for camping on the Ayres as it is not an official camp site, but that did not worry us, and we were glad that the lack of basic facilities meant that very few people camped there. We bought a small camper-van, which we would park as near to the Point as we could get. There Barbara would spot ships passing and relay their names to me; and I would usually be able to tell her what kind of vessel each was, where it was bound for and so on. By now, she, too, had developed an interest in the sea. We were also free to take the dogs on off-lead walks for hours as there are no roads on the Ayres and they could come to no harm. Sometimes we would go for twenty-four hours without making contact with another human being. At night I would nod off to sleep to the swish of the tide and the occasional background noise from the engine of a passing ship. In the winter months on the Ayres wind-speed would frequently get up to 80 or 90 miles per hour, and you would not be able to remain on your feet, but in the summer it was a haven of peace and tranquillity.

Before the days of the camper-van we had tried camping in a tent on the Ayres; this proved to be a complete disaster. At the time, we were living in St John's and we bought the tent with a view to taking

Camping on the Ayres. Experience showed that a camper-van was preferable to a tent in windy conditions.

An 'exclusive' Glassey photograph of the Emeraude light aircraft which was retrieved from the sea after ditching about one mile off the Point of Ayre in August, 1991.

ourselves and the dogs off for week-ends to the Point of Ayre. In our one and only attempt at camping in this wild and isolated area we pitched the tent in the most sheltered spot we could find. The first night went fine, but on the second day a gale sprang up and our lovely new, and up until now sturdy, tent began to behave like a drunken sailor. The gale lashed at its sides, ripping out the factory-manufactured tent pegs as if they were matches. In order to keep our tent intact the only thing we could do was to remain inside it and sit on the canvas walls. We both sat there for hours huddled against the wireless listening to the shipping forecasts and praying that the wind would abate. We were both becoming tired and weary and about to give up when the familiar voice of Geordie Adamson, my old friend the lighthouse keeper from the Calf of Man, filtered through the tent doorway. "Are you in trouble, Thomas?" He had now relocated to the Point of Ayre lighthouse, and on seeing our predicament he had taken himself off to his workshop and made us a complete set of new, much stronger, tent pegs. Within a few minutes, Geordie was hammering the still-hot pegs into the hard ground. At last, with our tent now secure, Barbara and I could relax and sleep easy and we went on to stay on the Ayres for about a week.

The drama was not over, however. A couple of days later a light aircraft on its way from the Island to Scotland came down in the sea about half a mile from the Point. The only person on board was the pilot who, for reasons known only to himself, refused to leave his sick but still floating plane. It is amazing how quickly word spreads whenever a dramatic event is taking place on the Island. In no time at all the normally quiet and isolated Ayres was full of folks who had all come over to watch the drama unfold. The Ramsey lifeboat was quickly on the scene but the reluctant pilot, who seemed to think he had some kind of insurance problem with regard to salvage or something, still refused to leave his plane and could be clearly seen sitting tight up there on its tail. Soon an air-sea rescue helicopter arrived from Anglesey and eventually the reluctant pilot left his plane, although I cannot recall whether it was on board the Ramsey lifeboat or in the helicopter. The plane was towed to the beach by the lifeboat and pulled ashore by the coastguard. It was a shame, really, as the pilot had performed wonders in landing his plane on the water only for the coastguard to turn it into a total write-off by the time they had finished dragging it over the stony beach. It was pulled up on to the grass and into the grounds of the lighthouse. The lighthouse gates were then locked and no one, not even the press photographers, was allowed near it. The following morning, Barbara and I rose early, about 4 a.m., and made our way to the lighthouse grounds. She knew I wanted to have a good feel of the plane but had not been allowed near it the night before. We climbed the wall, and with absolutely no one around, bar seabirds and rabbits, I spent a good half hour having a thorough examination of the aircraft. Barbara even took photographs of me standing next to the wrecked plane. By camping at the scene and rising early we had succeeded where the local press photographers had failed. The Ayres is a place with no resources whatsoever, yet we had managed to put in a very eventful and exciting week's holiday.

Chapter Twenty-eight

We had only been living in Ramsey for a few short months when my fortunes changed. I really didn't know where I might find employment, I was now 25 miles from Castletown, too far from Dad and his log-splitter, and I was by now well out of touch with engineering. There had been many advances with computerisation and so on, so the chances of getting back into any factory work seemed pretty bleak. The Isle of Man Government had recently appointed a new person, Jenny Shanley, to the post of disability officer. She had rung me as all the new ones did, and made the customary appointment. On the day of appointment I sat thinking to myself: "Here we go again. I am going to get another dose of the usual stuff such as 'The windows of opportunity are opening wider' and 'Have you considered taking on any voluntary work?' I was quite accustomed to that kind of lingo from these well-meaning people but I couldn't have been more wrong. Jenny duly turned up, not only full of enthusiasm, but also breathing real hope of future employment. She asked me if I would be interested in working for a bank. I laughed, as I knew absolutely nothing about banks or banking, The idea that I might actually work for one was a joke. She persuaded me that, even though I had absolutely no experience of banking, there was a chance that one of the banks on the Island might be willing to take me on as a telephonist. That seemed even funnier - I hardly knew what a switchboard was, let alone how to operate one. She asked me if she managed to fix up an interview, would I at least go through with it. "Of course," I said, still not believing that there would ever be such an interview. A few days later I received notice to be at the Royal Bank of Scotland in Douglas for an interview on a given date.

On the day of the interview I went along with Jenny to the board-room of the Royal Bank of Scotland to be interviewed by the company secretary, Mr Scot Girvan. The interview went along very nicely with Scot asking lots of questions and me answering "no" to them all. No, I knew nothing about banks. No, I had no experience of switch-boards. No, I would not be able to read or write any documents. In fact, I think the only time I said "yes" was when I was asked if I would be willing to undertake training. Jenny did a superb job in assuring the Royal Bank that support would be provided by the Government both for training and for the purchase of special equipment I had never even heard of. I left the Royal Bank feeling as though I had at least been through the motions; and I had enjoyed the experience. I was totally gobsmacked a couple of days later when the phone rang and Scot Girvan's voice at the other end of the phone informed me that I had got the job. Would I be ready to travel to Loughborough the following week for training?

Escort accompanied me to Loughborough, which was almost too good to be true. We flew to Birmingham on 15th March, 1992 and were driven by taxi from the airport to the college at Loughborough, all at the Royal Bank's expense. I felt like a king. A week later I returned to the Island knowing as much as you could learn about switchboards in a week, and duly reported for work at the Royal Bank of Scotland on Monday, 22nd March. Better still, Escort was also allowed into the bank and did not have to stay outside in one of those awful kennels.

Operating the Royal Bank of Scotland's switchboard meant that I got to speak to about 500 people a day, which meant that I made friends with people from all over the world. I was soon on first name terms with Americans, Indians, Australians, Africans and the Lord only knows who else. I quickly got to know various members of staff in other branches around the United Kingdom. Going to work each day was like going to a social club and never knowing which of my pals was going to walk in through the door next. I had a full-time job where I didn't get my hands dirty, wet or cold, and all I had to do was say "good morning" and be nice to people. This was not a job, it was

more like stealing money. Of course, Barbara working for the time-share firm in Ramsey meant that I had now to catch the half-past seven bus each morning from Ramsey to Douglas, and back again at five o'clock. This was ironic in view of the fact that we had moved from St John's to Ramsey in order to be nearer to work for Barbara. And so it was now me who had to do the travelling.

I guess no one wants to stand still, we always want to reach out and grab any new opportunities that might be out there. It was only a question of time in the Royal Bank before operating the switchboard would not be enough. Of course, I knew that not being able to read or write anything except in Braille was always going to be my biggest handicap. Barbara was very computer literate and always tried to keep abreast of whatever was on offer. For my part, I didn't even know what a computer was. I had never used one and had accepted that they were going to pass me by in this life. It was Barbara who eventually put an end to my computer-barren life. She finally discovered a system that would enable me to read any printed document, and also to be able to write as well. This system would convert any printed text into Braille, and vice versa. The big draw-back was the £8,000 it was going to cost. I approached the Royal Bank. Of course, they were very much in favour of a system that would enable me to be able to both read and write in just the same way as my colleagues and agreed to fund part of it, if the Department of Trade and Industry would fund the rest. It was Jenny Shanley who came to the rescue once again. I contacted her, and within a very short time the new equipment was on its way.

(Facing page) A Red Letter day in the life of the author was when he was provided with the latest computer technology which scans normal text and converts to a Braille print out. Here the author is in company with his colleagues, who are from left to right, Karin Kelly, Marilyn Lyman, Adele Kaighin, Mike Quayle (Manx Telecom), Scott Girvan, Ann Fletcher (Manx Blind Welfare Society) and Jenny Shanley (Department of Health and Social Security).

Chapter Twenty-nine

I have had many truly wonderful days in my life. The day I left school in Liverpool and sailed home to the Island was indeed a great day. The day I stood on the quay in Douglas after disembarking from the Steam Packet ferry with my first guide dog giving me independence and the freedom to come and go as I liked, was another great day. However, I think the most wonderful day of my life, apart from the day I married Barbara, was the day I turned on my lap-top computer. For the first time in forty-odd years I could read anything I wanted to, and not just those articles that were specially Brailled by the Royal National Institute for the Blind. The R.N.I.B. do a magnificent job, but of course they are always going to be limited in the amount of material they can produce. The freedom to be able to walk into any newsagents and select a magazine of my own choice was beyond belief. My first magazine was my all-time favourite, *Sea Breezes*. The system worked quite simply: I placed the magazine on a scanner and scanned in the document, which was then converted into Braille and printed on a Braille display attached to the lap-top in place of a screen, on which I could read the text. I could now write printed text as well. All I had to do was type out my text on the PC keyboard, the text appeared in Braille on the Braille display, but would be converted to normal printed text on the screen or if I sent it to a printer. The Royal Bank allowed me to take this equipment home at nights so I had the best of both worlds. I was able to use it so that I could read documents at work and then it was as if the lights all went on again as soon as I got home. Of course, I had a great deal to learn about computers and it's quite likely that had it not been for Barbara's persistence and teaching I would have gone through life computerless. I also had to learn how to spell in print.

Barbara continued to play with systems, constantly searching for anything new, and before long the next big break-through came: the Internet. For weeks, Barbara worked long into the night in a bid to make it possible for me to access the Internet. Then, one evening, after many frustrating hours, my Braille display burst into life and I was on the Internet. Barbara had sent out requests on the Internet for software for a Braille display using MS DOS. Everyone was using Windows at this time but Braille was behind the technology and DOS was the only medium Braille could use. Mike Bromich of Advanced Systems found some software that needed adapting, and with the help of the author in America I was able to go on-line. Being able to access the Internet meant I could now download newspapers and have even greater access to the world of print than the scanner gave me. Newspapers for various reasons cannot be scanned owing to their size and the type of print that is used. Going on the Internet meant that I could download a newspaper directly from the site, save it and read it when ready. I could also visit shipping sites and read nautical infor-mation that previously I had had no way of accessing. As far as print was concerned, I was now all but living in a sighted world.

Border Television became interested in my Internet surfing and sent a camera crew to record a five-minute slot for one of their news programmes. It may only have been a five minute slot, but it took a whole day to record. The filming had to start in the Royal Bank as they wanted to show how I used the equipment at work during the day; but then I packed it up and took it home to demonstrate how I surfed the Internet during the evenings. Of course, Barbara had spent days tidying and cleaning in preparation for their visit. When they arrived, they took an immediate interest in the models of various ships that I had collected over the years. In anticipation of this, we had polished up for their inspection the one we thought they would be most interested in - the largest of them, a model of the Steam Packet vessel *Victoria* - only for them to turn their attention to a model of the *Titanic* that Barbara had made from a plastic kit. It, of course, was berthed on the only shelf in the house she hadn't cleaned!

Computers were becoming more and more important to me, both

at home and at work. The next break-through at the Royal Bank was to get on to the Bank's main-frame. To do this we needed the help of the Government once again, and once again it was forthcoming. The idea of Government funding or part-funding is twofold: firstly, it leaves people for whom the funding is provided free to leave a company, taking the equipment with them so that they can continue to earn a living elsewhere; and secondly, it means that the company does not incur huge costs as a result of taking on a disabled person. My new computer system, which used the most up-to-date Windows software, meant that I was not restricted just to operating the Bank's switchboard but could handle basic enquiries such as giving out account balances and so on. I owe the Royal Bank of Scotland and my wife, Barbara, a great debt of gratitude for their persistence in getting me involved with computers. For without them this book certainly would never have been written; and there would have been lots of books that would never have been read - not by me, anyway!

Unemployment soon came Barbara's way as the time-share company she worked for shed a large number of its staff, due to a take-over by another company. She wasn't out of work long and soon found employment as a programmer with a software firm in Douglas. This meant that the two of us now were living in Ramsey and commuting the 15 miles to and from Douglas every day. It no longer made sense to carry on living there and the search duly started for a house back in Castletown. We had had five happy years in Ramsey. The people of Ramsey had been marvellous. They had treated me as one of their own and I would miss them for sure. I would also miss The Swan, which had become my local pub, and its landlord, Alan Christian, better known as Mousy, who had become a great friend. At the same time, it was really nice to be going home to Castletown once again.

We had no difficulty selling our bungalow in Ramsey, but finding a house in Castletown proved extremely difficult, so much so that we had to take a house in Port St Mary for a year while we waited for one to become available in Castletown. This was no great hardship; I had

(Facing Page) A recent photograph of the author, seated, with his colleagues who handle hundreds of calls each day through the switchboard of the Royal Bank of Scotland International. They are, from left to right, Gemma Johnson, Clare Sibbald, Julie Moy, Martin Bailey, Alan Gelling, James Collier and Julie Jones.

always been fond of Port St Mary, and I had, in the past, often walked over from Castletown with Waldo. After ten months a house finally became available in Castletown. We placed our small house in Port St Mary on the market and sold it the same day. A couple of months later we moved to Kinfare on Victoria Road, and once again I was back home in Castletown. I re-named the house Ben Ellan after the small Ramsey Steam Ship steamer that I had spent so much time aboard as a child while she was being discharged in Castletown. My close affinity with the Steam Packet and the Ramsey Steam Ship Company remains as strong as ever. Over the years I have collected and commissioned the building of many models of Steam Packet ships. In 1997, the Steam Packet launched their latest vessel, the ro-pax vessel, *Ben-my-Chree*. Like all new ships, and especially passenger ferries that operate single-ship routes, she got a fair amount of flack from the general public. I have never sailed on the new *Ben-my-Chree* and, indeed, I am as guilty as anyone of jumping on the bandwagon and joining the masses in their condemnation of this ship. She is not the type of vessel that endears herself to me as from my own point of view, your shoes are far too far from the water. I would think her crew probably has more of a problem with low cloud than high seas but, be that as it may, she has now more or less completely overcome her early teething problems and is proving to be a fine seaworthy vessel. Nonetheless, during her early and troublesome days, I did join all those who had little regard for her and I wrote this poem:

I'm lying here in Douglas, once again I did not sail.
The Island's got no papers, and Marksies' bread's gone stale.
I'm a brand new ship from Holland, and Ben-my-Chree's my
*   name.*
I'm the slowest ship they ever built, and I've other claims to fame.
I watch my little sister, The Lady, pass me by.
She's on her way to Liverpool, so why the hell can't I.
She is 25 years my senior, and only half my size,
But I mustn't go out there today, for fear I might capsize.
I see the yachts out in the Bay, with all their sails unfurled.
My Chairman's told my passengers, I can sail anywhere in the
*   world.*
To Tokyo or Sidney, or even Santa Fe,

But Liverpool or Heysham, is just too far away.
I lie here in the harbour, feeling so uneasy.
My sailings have been cancelled because it is too breezy.
I'm storm-bound here in Douglas, and on my berth I lie.
It really is embarrassing as a canoe goes paddling by.
I've got another sister, she's called a Super Cat.
She takes day-trippers to Liverpool but doesn't bring them back.
The Lady comes to the rescue, she always is on call.
I avoid these situations by not leaving port at all.
Now we've got a little system, it really is unique.
It protects us from the elements, when the weather is too bleak.
My Captain lights a candle, and hangs it from my railings,
And if the wind doth blow it out, he cancels all my sailings.

It was written one day purely for my own amusement and that night I took my one and only copy around to the pub with me. The first person to read it asked me if he could keep it and, of course, I said yes. That was that as far as I was concerned. However, the next day the poem's new owner took it to work with him and faxed it to someone else, who photocopied it and sent it elsewhere. Within a couple of days just about everyone in Douglas was walking around with a copy of it. Soon, Manx Radio received a copy and started to broadcast it. Then the local newspaper printed the poem. It now hangs in shops, bars and cafés all over the Island. On most of the copies the poem is unattributed, as it was never my intention to publish it. However, now I will put the record straight and hold my hands up. The Steam Packet has been a life-long friend to me right from child-hood, and no one likes to kick a friend in the teeth - and I must admit it did feel a little bit like that as the poem's distribution gathered momentum. I include this lament to the *Ben-my-Chree* now so it can finally be put to bed, and I guess no one can be forgiven for his or her sins until they admit guilt.

I hope that with Barbara's help I went some way to repaying the Steam Packet for my *Ben-my-Chree* lament. The year 1999 was the 90th anniversary of the loss of the *Ellan Vannin*, a Steam Packet ship which had sunk in 1909 with the loss of all 37 persons on board. We both wanted to mark this occasion by doing something, and so with Barbara's musical talent and my having a go at the lyrics we attempted to write a song. Neither of us had ever tried song-writing before, and we had absolutely no idea about what was involved in trying to record one. Once I had written the words, it didn't take Barbara long to conjure up a tune. To set it to music we enlisted the help of a lady by the name of Anita J. who is a well-known entertainer and singer around the Island. We more or less threw the song at her and she duly came up with the goods. Now it was time to record it. Barbara and I had no idea how you went about this so we just rang up a recording studio and booked it for the day. I guess it was a bit of good luck on our part that we just happened to have booked a studio owned by Mark Cleator.

We turned up on the day with nothing more than a keyboard and a sheet of paper with the words of the song. We had no other backing or instruments. Apart from Barbara's cornet-playing, neither of us played anything. Of course, Anita had provided us with some backing but as we were to discover we needed much more than a keyboard and a singer. Mark Cleator is a musician in his own right, and in order for us to come away with a recording of our song we had to call on all his skills, and a few more I don't think he knew he had. At the end of the day we did end up with a recording of a song called 'Ellan Vannin Remembered', which was what we had set out to achieve in the first place. I doubt we would have attempted this if we had known what was involved. A lot of the credit for the song must go to Barbara who

168

had never sung in a recording studio before and managed to record the song in only about two takes. It's probably something we will never do again, but we did enjoy the experience. Although the CD only ever went on sale in Castletown Post Office, where our good friend, John Saunders, sold over 300 copies, I hope it went a little way towards repaying the Steam Packet for my attack on their *Ben-my-Chree* a year earlier. The idea of the CD was simply to mark the 90th anniversary of the sinking of the *Ellan Vannin*, and I guess in a small way we managed to achieve that. Richard Stafford, of course, marked the occasion much more fittingly with his book, "The *Ellan Vannin* Story".

I am really lucky to have Barbara, who is the inspiration behind most things I do, and shares my love of the Island. It is a wonderful feeling being back, and now permanently, in the little town I love so much, and I guess the strength of my love for the place was born out of those days when, as a small child, I had no alternative but to leave it. I intend now to spend the rest of my days here. I don't even have an inclination to go on holiday to any far-off places since I know I could not be as happy anywhere else as I am here.

Today, my Dad, at seventy-three years old, still sets off for work every morning on his tractor to manage an estate on the Ballamodha Straight. Mother, at seventy-two, still works in a local hotel. My brother, Lenny, with his wife Rosie, now runs a quarry in Poyllvaaish, just south of Castletown. My younger brother, Sean, works in the quarry with Lenny. Uncle Normie, who I guested with at week-ends in Coventry, now runs an estate on Fisher's Hill, just outside Castletown. Michael is still fishing with his two sons out of Castletown. Captain Jack Ronan is now retired and lives in Castletown. I am still with the Royal Bank of Scotland, operating the switchboard and dealing with customer enquiries. My wife, Barbara, now works for Zurich Financial Services in Douglas as a Senior Analyst/Programmer. We still have Escort, though we lost our lovely blue-eyed collie, Bess, to cancer last year.

Every day we both set off from Castletown in the car, and as we turn left on to the main road, there is never a day goes by when I don't think back to those days when so often I made that left turn to face the despair of leaving this little town and heading off to Douglas to catch the nine o'clock boat for Liverpool. I owe a great deal indeed to my family and friends who have helped me along the way from those sad days when we had to be parted. I hope this book serves as a tribute and a thank you to all those who helped, from those early days right up to the present day. If I had not had such a wonderful family and friends, there would not have been such heartache back in those dark days. Of course, my biggest vote of thanks must go to my wife, Barbara. For if she had not pushed me along and encouraged me to write this book and acted as my IT support, the book would never have been written.

I have always loved my Island home, with its special magic and its friendly people. It is a place which I have never feared and where I will never be afraid of the dark.

Together with Bess on Langness, where the author enjoys nothing more than the sound of the waves and the call of the birds.

Postscript

In September 2000, the opportunity arose for me to purchase my own boat, the *Sea Dancer* which is a 25 foot, twin-engined fibre-glass vessel. She was berthed in Peel, the main seaport on the west coast of the Island. After I had carried out a brief inspection of the boat and consulted with my seafaring friends, I readily parted with the agreed sale price for the vessel.

On Saturday the 25th September at 7 a.m., I arrived on Peel breakwater where the *Sea Dancer* was berthed, having been driven there from Castletown by Barbara, my wife. Michael Quine had spent the previous night on board my newly-acquired boat and it was only fitting that Michael, my lifelong friend, should skipper her around the coast to Castletown, a journey of some 17 miles or so. We had waited for several weeks for a break in the weather to allow us to complete this final stage. The *Sea Dancer* would have a crew of four for this sailing - Michael as acting skipper, myself as owner, Tony Hanrahan, an old friend and seadog, and Alan Cregeen who was on holiday from Canada and staying in Castletown. The only down side was that Barbara would not be able to make the trip around, as someone had to look after the dogs and chickens back home. Nonetheless it did mean we had someone on hand to take the photos of our grand arrival back in Castletown.

Our journey around the coast took us four hours. This was somewhat longer than we had anticipated as our starboard engine started to overheat some 20 minutes out of Peel. This meant that we had to manage largely on our port engine which had just been rebuilt and was in the process of being run in. As we entered Castletown harbour I could

feel a lump rising in my throat and a tear welling in my eyes. I was sailing into Castletown aboard my own boat! I thought of how many times as a child I had been taken out by other boatmen and of how I had dreamed of one day owning my own boat. It had taken around 40 years for the dream to be realised, but this day it had been fulfilled. As we drew level with the pier Alan, our Canadian crew member, gave three long blasts on *Sea Dancer's* air whistle and Barbara stood on the quay snapping with the camera as we slowly inched our way up the harbour. Michael eventually secured *Sea Dancer* on a berth in the upper part of Castletown harbour where she will now remain for the rest of the winter, well out of the reach of the winter's southwesterly gales. It was a truly wonderful and proud day for me.

———————

Another very proud day for me was Saturday, 25th November. On this day I made my first trip back to St. Vincent's School for the Blind in Liverpool since leaving in 1969. I took the Saturday day trip on the Steam Packet vessel *Lady of Mann*. It was a very stormy day and there was a real possibility that the return sailing from Liverpool might be cancelled. Fortunately this did not happen and although it was a fairly lively trip, I had sailed in worse conditions in years gone by. Of course I could have flown, but I wanted to try and relive those days so long ago when I had made these sailings as a child. This time I was going back to school of my own choice, however, and as the *Lady of Mann* slowed down and crept up the Mersey, the memory of those sad and tearful days all came flooding back to me. It was a very strange feeling as I stepped from the gangway on to the floating landing stage in Liverpool in the pouring rain.

The Pier Head is no longer the hive of activity that it used to be. I had intended to ride out to the school on the bus, just as I had done all those years ago with mum or dad. However, the buses no longer run from the Pier Head. I had only a few hours to spend in Liverpool and did not have time to waste searching for buses and so decided to take a taxi. I wondered just how Mother and Father must have felt 33

The author, standing at the rear, savours the proud moment of entering Castletown harbour in his own boat 'Sea Dancer'. With him, in the bows, is old friend Tony Hanrahan, at the helm is acting skipper, Michael Quine, and Alan 'Copper' Cregeen is keeping a lookout.

years ago when they were placed in the same situation as I was now. The difference being from their point of view was that they often had no option of taking a taxi. Money being the way it was in those days, meant that they had to struggle on and find the right bus even though their time was more limited than mine. As the taxi made the left turn into what used to be that old gravely driveway at St. Vincent's, it was almost as if I had turned the clock back some 30 odd years. The gravel has now gone from the driveway and been replaced by a smooth tarmac finish. The front doors of St. Vincent's were exactly the same, even the bell seemed to make an old and worn out sound. I passed through those big front doors and stepped immediately onto the highly polished tiled floor of the front hallway. I had not smelt that polish for over 30 years. Everything appeared to be more or less exactly as I had left it.

My host for the day was one of the present teachers, Paul Mannings, a very likeable chap who had given up his Saturday afternoon and opened the school especially for me. Paul explained that the school was no longer run by the nuns, and in order to remain in existence St Vincent's was now open to children of all religious denominations.

All the children now go home at weekends which meant that the school was empty for my visit. It was almost as if the school had stood still in a time warp. The building certainly had, and everything was more or less the way I had left it. The long corridors still echoed as I walked along them, and it felt as though a hundred years of history oozed from the tiled walls. It was those walls that had for so long been the barrier between home and me. But I have much to be grateful for as I realised what St Vincent's had done for me. It is the foundation of my story and probably the foundation of my well-being today. I am sure that the school is no longer an awesome prospect facing a young child of today, although I am sure there is still the odd tear-stained pillow belonging to a child on a Monday night who probably feels that Friday is a lifetime away.

As I left the school I was gladdened to know that blind children of today are in the enlightened care of Paul Mannings and his colleagues, under Headteacher Mr Anthony MacQuarrie. It is also good to know that St Vincent's continues to shine as a beacon of light for those who will need its guidance in the future.

ST VINCENT'S SCHOOL TODAY

Under the auspices of the Catholic Blind Institute, St Vincent's first opened its doors in 1901 to receive children who were blind or partially sighted. Today, it is regarded as a centre of excellence catering for children from the age of 4 to 17 years of age on a daily or weekly residential basis. The ethos of the school is to provide a caring atmosphere with Christian values to foster mutual respect, individual achievement and self reliance so that they can fully integrate into society. This is achieved by

a dedicated and qualified staff whose numbers provide a high staff to pupil ratio. The pupils have access to the National Curriculum at all levels leading to a wide range of recognised academic awards up to G.C.S.E. In addition there is training in mobility and living skills and the school has full medical care. The many extra curricular activities include educational visits, field trips and Duke of Edinburgh Awards.

Individual careers guidance and work experience leads to Higher Education and employment, enabling pupils to train for telephony, office and social work, computer programming and information technology,

teaching and law, piano tuning, catering, hotel management and hospital radio.

St Vincent's is a non-maintained school of charitable status and is partly funded by fees received from Local Education Authorities whose children are placed in the school. There is also great reliance on fund raising to equip the school with the many extras for the benefit of its pupils. Parents and interested people and commercial con-

cerns all contribute to this. As a result, the classrooms are well equipped and there are C.C.T.Vs, computers with speech synthesisers and large print facility. Staff keep fully abreast with the latest in Braille software. Blind children develop literacy skills through Braille from the earliest years. The school has specialist rooms for Science, Art, Information/Design and Food Technology, a Business Centre and a Library. There is also a Music Department offering a wide range of instruments, and a new music technology studio. Sports facilities include a running track, playing fields, an all-weather pitch, assault course and a heated swimming pool. The school is proud to represent Britain in International athletic events.

"This is a very good school that serves its pupils well."

- OFSTED Report.